Emir Muʿāwiyah

and

Medieval Chroniclers and Traditionalists

By Two Contemporary Scholars

Dr Syed Ridwan ʻAli Nadwi

& Shaykh Hassan Bin ʻAli Al Saqqaf Al Hashimi Al Husayni

Rendered Into English

By Khusro Qasim and Sayyid Asad Amir Dean Husayni

First Printing, 2020
ISBN 978-1-7752492-7-6

Acknowledgement

I am very grateful for getting the opportunity to work with Assistant Professor Khusro Qasim in bringing his vast research on Ahl al- Bayt and related topics that are most critically required in the English-speaking world. We will continue to translate his works so the immense research will benefit generations to come and will reconnect our Ummah with the noble house of the Prophet Muhammad ﷺ.

Sayyid Asad Amir Dean Husayni

Toronto, Canada

PREFACE

We have embarked on publishing this book as an anecdote to a rampant virus spreading that includes praising highly questionable figures whose life objective was to trouble the members of the Prophet Muhammad's ﷺ family and their companions. My father studied with the late Shaykh Abul Hasan Al Nadwi and hence we are producing the work from his prestigious institution. On a personal note, I have attached to the school of the great scholars of Morocco the Ghumari masters via one of my teachers Shaykh Muhammad bin Yahya Al Ninowy so hence the English work of Shaykh Hassan Al Saqqaf.

Recently groups have risen up in places that are eulogizing Mu'awaiyah and are looking to even build mosques, etc. This is largely due to sheer ignorance and sectarian and dogmatic doctrines. While the position has traditionally been to remain silent as instructed by our grandfathers including the great Shaykh Abdul Qadir Jilani of Baghdad, we have been compelled to come out with these works in English so that this goes back to becoming a silent position not worth discussing.

Sayyid Asad Amir Dean Husayni

FOREWORD

In the Name of Allah, the Beneficent, the Merciful

Since late, Nāṣibiyat has reached its height of influence and its agents have infiltrated the ranks of Ahl al-Sunnah in such a way, that their poisonous effects have abominably affected the beliefs of the general populace.

As a result, people have begun to view Emir Mu'āwiyah as an equal of 'Ali and have started to compare both personalities with each other. Considering the delicateness of the subject at hand, Dr Ridhwan Nadwi wrote an article which was published in Pakistan a long time ago. Due to the article's significant relevancy in present times, we are now publishing it in book form. Dr Ridhwan Nadwi has graduated from India's most prestigious school of knowledge, Darul 'Uloom, Nadwat al-'Ulama, Lucknow. During the 50's, he was studying Arabic and Islamic Sciences in the Sharia College of Mecca and Damascus University. After receiving a Ph.D. from Britain, he taught for two years in Saudi Arabia's Islamic University, and fourteen years in Libya's Benghazi University. Quite a few of his published works in Arabic and Urdu have gained widespread popularity.

It is my prayer unto Allah that may He inspire me to defend the cause of Ahl al-Bayt and 'Ali till my last breath – Amen.

Khusro Qasim

Assistant Professor

Mechanical Engineering Department

AMU, 'Aligarh

CONTENTS

In the Name of Allah, the Beneficent, the Merciful

Emir Muʿāwiyah and Medieval Chroniclers and Traditionalists

All literate Muslims know that Emir Muʿāwiyah was a Companion of the Prophet Muhammad ﷺ. Perhaps only those who have deeply perused Islamic history shall know the intricacies of this man's life. This is not something which commoners shall know. After hearing about Emir Muʿāwiyah from the imams of Defense Society's two masjids during Friday sermons, I asked them, 'When did Muʿāwiyah accept Islam?' Both were unaware. Not many a man knows that Muʿāwiyah is most famous for being the founder of Islam's first Sultanate, the Kingdom of Banu Umayyah, better known as the Umayyad Sultanate. This is why medieval traditionalists and chroniclers have written about him in great detail. Since the official syllabus does not include Islamic History as a subject, Moulvis graduating from universities (who later become Maulānas and Muftis) also do not know about the life of Emir Muʿāwiyah.

On Sunday, 2nd June, an article written by a 'scholar' Aurangzeb Farooqi was published in 'Ummat'. It was titled, Syedna Emir Muʿāwiyah'. The author had recounted therein the virtues and laudable deeds of Emir Muʿāwiyah. It appears from this article that not only has the author ignored the writings of medieval traditionalists and chroniclers, but has also willfully avoided Quranic verses pertaining to the honourable Companions. At least I do not know of any writings in Arabic or Urdu which may have been authored by this 'scholar'. For me, those who deserve the title of 'scholar' are persons like Maulāna Syed Noor Shah Kashmiri, Maulāna Shabbir Ahmad Usmani, Maulāna Syed Sulaiman Nadwi, Maulāna Syed Abul Hasan 'Ali Nadwi, Dr Muhammad Hamidullah and other such eminent personalities, who all have written tens of books on Islamic subjects in Arabic and Urdu. As for Dr Muhammad Hamidullah, he has authored a substantial amount of material about the hagiography of the Prophet Muhammad ﷺ, and general Islamic history in English also. That the aforementioned author, following in the style of a particular Islamic sect to which belong all officiators of religious congregations and Moulvis, has chosen for his self the title of 'scholar' all by himself is another thing altogether.

Nevertheless, when we begin to read the content of the article, we realize that the author deeply loves Emir Muʿāwiyah. Loving him is his right but twisting historical facts and presenting them in a concocted manner is in no way a proper thing to do. This article which you are currently reading has been written with the sole objective of providing the readers with factual and truthful information which they can apprise themselves of, without having to lean towards partisan and one-sided opinions and preferences.

The author has commenced his article thus: "Emir Mu'āwiyah was a highly respected Companion of the Prophet Muhammad ﷺ, a caliph of great stature, writer of Divine Revelation and its guardian, confidant of the Prophet Muhammad ﷺ, and a close advisor to 'Umar Fārūq and ʿUthmān Ghanī. This is why he held top positions during the caliphates of Abu Bakr, 'Umar and ʿUthmān."

These words are contrary to the fact. If it was only Emir Mu'āwiyah who was a 'highly respected Companion and a caliph of great stature', then what words of praise remain for Abu Bakr,

Umar Fārūq and 'Ali? The Quran has delivered its verdict regarding the Companions of the Prophet Muhammad ﷺ, and their ranks and that verdict is binding. Allah the Almighty states in Surah al-Ḥadīd, 'Those who spent and fought before the victory are not upon a level (with the rest of you). Such are greater in rank than those who spent and fought afterwards. Unto each hath Allah promised good' [57:10]. It has been proven through historical fact that Emir Mu'āwiyah accepted Islam after the victory of Mecca. According to 'Allamah Ibn Taimiyah and 'Allamah Dahabi, he, his father and his brother Yazīd bin Abu Sufyān were among those who were manumitted (Ṭuluqā) and were paid money so that they would not leave the fold of Islam (Whose hearts were to be reconciled 9:60). The Ṭuluqā were those Meccans who, according to Arabian laws of warfare, could have been made captives and slaves but the Prophet Muhammad ﷺ, said to those terrified Meccans, 'Go, for you all are manumitted' Thence they were freed. References are provided in subsequent pages.

Furthermore, Mu'āwiyah is not among those who were the 'First to lead the way, of the Muhājirīn and the Anṣār' [9:100], for whom Allah the Almighty sent down glad tidings; and neither is he among those who 'Followed in goodness' those who were the 'First to lead,' meaning — before the victory of Mecca. This is because after the victory of Mecca, Islam spread across Arabia and became ubiquitous among the numerous tribes merely based on its might. Whereupon, those having accepted Islam after the victory of Mecca were not at par, as regards their position and stature, with those who had submitted to the message of Islam before the victory of Mecca.

Allah the Almighty then recalled them stating, 'And the foremost in the race; the foremost in the race: Those are they who will be brought nigh' [56:10-11]. He thereby affirmed their lofty status through the epithet 'Foremost' which He bestowed upon them.

Now who are these people who were brought nigh unto their Lord? They are: Abu Bakr, ʻUmar, ʿUthmān, ʻAli, Abu ʻUbaidah, Saʿad bin Abi Waqqāṣ, Zubair bin ʿAwām, ʿAbd al-Raḥmān bin ʿAwf, Ṭalḥah, Saʿīd bin Zaid bin ʻUmar, "the ten" who were promised paradise; meaning those Companions to whom the Prophet Muhammad ﷺ, delivered glad tidings about them entering paradise. Others who are the ʻForemost' are Yāsir, his wife Sumayyah, his son ʿAmmār, Bilāl, Ṣuhaib, Arqam, ʿAbdullah bin Masʿūd, Khālid bin Saʿīd, Zaid bin Ḥārithah, Ḥamzah, Jaʿfar, Abu Zar and other scores of Companions who can be included in this list. These are ones who should be described as ʻhighly respected and of great stature'. After them are the Anṣār of Medina who extended assistance and refuge to those who submitted to Islam at the behest of the Messenger of Allah ﷺ they extended refuge to Islam itself. Among them are Saʿad bin Muʿāz, Asyad bin Huḍayr, Muʿāẓ bin Jabal, ʿUbādah bin al-Ṣāmit, Ubay bin Kaʿab, Zaid bin Thābit and other scores of Anṣār. Due to their sacrifices and the assistance they provided to the Muhājirīn did Islam survive, and history is witness to their lofty ranks. These ranks do not belong to those who accepted Islam after the victory of Mecca and after having been subdued through losses inflicted upon them in tens of battles.

The ʻscholar' in question is clearly in error when he claims that Emir Mu'āwiyah was a close advisor to ʻUmar bin al-Khaṭṭāb. When ʻUmar saw him enter clad in green clothes, he struck him with his whip. When his companions enquired the cause for such a whiplashing, he pointed towards the sky and said, ʻI wished to mitigate his sense of lordliness.' Narrations of Ibn Kathīr and others contain the word ʻSha-ma-kha' (شمخ) which means lordliness (Ibn Kathīr: al-Bidāyah wal Nihāyah 8/125; Ibn Ḥajar: al-Iṣābah 434/3). Ibn Kathīr and Ibn Ḥajar have already narrated that when ʻUmar saw Muʿāwiyah, he used to say: ʻThis is the Khosrow of Arabs.' How then can he be a close advisor to ʻUmar?

The fact is when his half elder brother Yazīd bin Abu Sufyān was sent by Abu Bakr to conquer Syria and Palestine, the latter commissioned four armies under his command and Emir Mu'āwiyah was the commander in one of those armies. Yazīd died in the year 18 AH during the outbreak of the bubonic plague in Syria. As a result, 'Umar appointed his younger brother Muʿāwiyah, who had been with Yazīd in his army as his assistant, governor of Damascus. He did not hold any other high rank except this. It would be an exaggeration to say that he held top posts during the caliphate of Abu Bakr. No such thing has been narrated in any authentic and trustworthy book of history, be it in Urdu or Arabic. Imam Bukhāri and Imam Muslim have narrated the virtues and deeds of many honourable Companions of the Prophet Muhammad ﷺ and dedicated chapters to each of them, but they too have written nothing about the virtues of Emir Muʿāwiyah.

The author has also provided an incorrect account of Emir Muʿāwiyah's year of birth. It is correct that Ibn Kathīr and Ibn Ḥajar have indeed written that Mu'āwiyah was born five years before the Prophet Muhammad ﷺ, but the aforementioned author has provided a Gregorian year 608 AD which is incorrect. The correct date should be 605 AD because Muḥammad ﷺ, attained Prophethood in the Gregorian year 610 AD and this is a known fact. Furthermore, to provide a Gregorian date and cite references from Ibn Ḥajar's Kitāb al-Iṣābah and Ibn Kathīr's al-Bidāyah wal Nihāyah is pointless since these books do not provide Gregorian dates.

Concerning Muʿāwiyah's accepting Islam, he writes: "Emir Muʿāwiyah formally accepted Islam during the victory of Mecca but he had already submitted to the message of Islam well before that. Therefore, famous chronicler Wāqidī says: 'Ḥazrat Muʿāwiyah became a Muslim on the day of the Ḥudaybiyah Treaty but he concealed it and later declared it publicly on the day of the victory of Mecca." The respected author does not provide any citation for Wāqidī's quoted narration. In reality, Ibn Saʿad (230 AH) has written regarding Muʿāwiyah in his book Kitāb al-Ṭabaqāt al-Kubrā (Vol 7, p. 406) that he accepted Islam in the year of the Treaty of Ḥudaybiyah and concealed it from his father, later declaring it publicly on the day of the victory of Mecca. This is the narration of Ibn Saʿad and not Wāqidī. Additionally, the narration mentions the year of the Treaty of Ḥudaybiyah and not the exact day.

Likewise, Maulāna Aurangzeb has written a personal account of Muʿāwiyah narrated by himself on the authority of Ibn Saʿad where he [Muʿāwiyah] said, 'I accepted Islam on the day of ʿUmrat al-Qaḍā but concealed it fearing my father. I kept it concealed till the day of the victory of Mecca.' The reference provided here by the author is from Volume 8, page 118 of al-Bidāyah wal Nihāyah. This narration from Ibn Saʿad is not at all present on the given page of the book cited. It is on the 117th page of the 8th Volume where the author of the book Ibn Kathīr himself has written an apparently weak and unsubstantiated narration that begins with, 'And it has been narrated from him [Muʿāwiyah]' (عنه وروي) which then goes on to mention the narration provided above. Unfortunately, the author was not able to see the following narration which has been chronicled right after Muʿāwiyah's name and which says, 'Muʿāwiyah accepted Islam in the year of the victory of Mecca' (ال ف تح عام معاوية ا سلم). This means that it has been narrated from Emir Muʿāwiyah himself that he accepted Islam one year prior to the victory of Mecca on the occasion of ʿUmrat al-Qaḍā, i.e. 7 AH whereas Ibn Saʿad has written in his book Kitāb al-Ṭabaqāt al-Kubrā that Muʿāwiyah narrated that he accepted Islam in the year of the Treaty of Ḥudaybiyah. These are contradictory narrations and according to the Arabic principles of narration, when two reports contradict each other, they both are considered unworthy of acceptance (اذا ضا ناق ت ساقطا ت).

Therefore, both reports in question are not worthy to be considered authentic.

Emir Muʿāwiyah as such did not accept Islam in the year of the Treaty of Ḥudaybiyah i.e. 6 AH nor on the occasion of the ʿUmrat al-Qaḍā. Rather, it is as Wāqidī and Ibn Saʿad have narrated elsewhere that he accepted Islam on the day of the victory of Mecca. In his book Ṭabaqāt, Ibn Saʿad has narrated in a chapter in Volume 4 (p. 389-392) entitled 'Companions who accepted Islam before the victory of Mecca' the biographies of 143 companions which does not contain the name of Muʿāwiyah. This means that Muʿāwiyah accepted Islam only after the victory of Mecca. The author has erred in what he writes that, "Sheikh al-Islam Ḥāfiẓ Ibn Ḥajar says that Muʿāwiyah bin Abu Sufyān was a companion of the Prophet Muhammad ﷺ, and a rightly guided caliph. He became honoured by Islam before the victory of Mecca." Neither is this report present in Ibn Ḥajar's more comprehensive Kitāb al-Iṣābah fi Tamyeez al-Ṣaḥābah, nor it can be located in his shorter Mukhtaṣar Kitāb Taqrīb al-Tahzīb. The reference cited by the author is incorrect. Then a further claim that the book al-Iṣābah contains a detailed biography of Muʿāwiyah and this book is a trustworthy source of history. Contrary to the claim of the author, Wāqidī (who is considered a liar by all traditionalists) has been criticized thus: Wāqidī's narration of Emir Muʿāwiyah accepting Islam before the victory of Mecca is refuted per se by Bukhāri and Muslim's narration about Saʿad bin Abi Waqqāṣ' report regarding the performing of ʿUmrah during the season of Ḥaj which is as follows: Sa'ad bin Abi Waqqāṣ said, "We performed the ʿUmrah and he [Muʿāwiyah] was an infidel at the time." (al-Iṣābah 3/433) (continued).

The most important statement in this regard has been made by Ḥāfiẓ ibn al-Qayyim who said: 'And there is no conflict [among historians] that Muʿāwiyah entered the fold of Islam on the occasion of the victory of Mecca in year 8 AH.' Ḥāfiẓ ibn al-Qayyim's teacher Ibn Taimiyah has written his Majmūʿah Fatāwā and Minhāj al-Sunnah as has been narrated in all books detailing the hagiography of the Prophet Muhammad ﷺ, that Muʿāwiyah, his brother Yazīd bin Abu Sufyān and their father were among the Ṭulaqā and those whose hearts were to be reconciled. From the booty of the Battle of Ḥunayn, the Prophet Muhammad ﷺ, gave each of them 100 camels and 40 [illegible] of silver (dirhams) like was given to other such leaders so that they would not leave the fold of Islam. If Emir Muʿāwiyah had indeed accepted Islam during the Treaty of Ḥudaybiyah (6 AH) or even at the time of ʿUmrat al-Qaḍā (7 AH), then he would not have received what he did from the war booty and the Prophet Muhammad ﷺ, would not have bestowed camels and silver upon him; and even if he did, then Muʿāwiyah should not have accepted it. And then was there any other companion who hid his Islam fearing his parents or master? Bilāl, ʿAmmār, Ṣuhayb and other companions suffered grave injustice but they persevered and did not hide their Islam. To say that he accepted Islam before the victory of Mecca in the sixth or seventh year after the Hijra is something which completely contradicts history and tradition. He [Muʿāwiyah] has been classified as being among those whose hearts were to be reconciled by Ibn Hishām in his Sīrah (Vol 4, p. 394), Ibn Khuzām in his Jawāmiʿ al-Sīrah (p. 245), Ibn Kathīr in al-Bidāyah wal Nihāyah (4/360) and others. Similarly, the reference of al-Iṣābah cited in the article which claims that Emir Muʿāwiyah was the writer of Divine Revelation is incorrect. One who wishes can read the biography of Muʿāwiyah in the third volume of Ḥāfiẓ Ibn Ḥajar's book. Nowhere in that book has Muʿāwiyah been described as the writer of Divine Revelation. This claim has been wrong publicized among people and, unfortunately, Ḥāfiẓ Ibn Kathīr has also gone with the flow. As far as Ḥāfiẓ Ibn Ḥajar is concerned, he is more knowledgeable than Ibn Kathīr and a more comprehensive traditionalist and chronicler than him. He, as like all other books of history, has written just this: 'And he [Mu῾āwiyah] wrote for him [The Prophet Muhammad ﷺ (لـه وک تب] Note that nowhere has it been mentioned that he wrote Divine Revelation. In the same book (al-Iṣābah) it has been narrated (3/434) on the authority of the very senior chronicler al-Madāinī (d. 225 AH) that, Zaid bin Thābit used to write Divine Revelation and Mu῾āwiyah used to write about the Prophet Muhammad's ﷺ, affairs concerning the Arabs.'Meaning, he used to write letters and agreements of the Prophet Muhammad ﷺ, The same has been written by Imam Ẓahabī, one hundred years before Ibn Ḥajar, in his detailed biography of Emir Mu῾āwiyah where he says: 'And he [Mu῾āwiyah] wrote for him [The Prophet Muhammad ﷺ] a few times.' (Siyar A῾lām al-Nubalā, al-Dahabī, Vol 3, p. 321)

One of the earliest chroniclers Abu al-Ḥasan al-Madāinī's book regarding the writers of Divine Revelation is lost. But a book written by another early chronicler Ibn ῾Abdūsh al-Jahshyārī regarding viziers and secretaries of Islam entitled al-Wuzarā wal Kuttāb is already published. In that book, the very first chapter is about secretaries working for the Prophet Muhammad ﷺ, during his lifetime. Along with their short descriptions, their expertise and area of work has also been narrated. It is as though a description of the Prophet Muhammad's ﷺ, own secretaries and office staff. In the list of those who wrote Divine Revelation are the names of 'Ali, ῾Uthmān, Ubay bin Ka῾ab and Zaid bin Thābit. It has also been mentioned further that Zaid bin Thābit used to write letters on behalf of the Prophet Muhammad ﷺ, to kings and rulers. As for Khālid bin Sa῾īd bin al-῾Āṣ and Emir Mu῾āwiyah, they used to write matters about daily routine. It should be noted that Muḥammad bin ῾Abdūsh al-Jahshyārī himself was a secretary under the Abbasids during the late third century Hijri and the first quarter of the fourth century. He died in 331 AH. As regards Ḥāfiẓ Ibn Ḥajar, he has written about Mu῾āwiyah in the seventh volume of his famous commentary of the Ṣaḥīḥ Bukhāri entitled Fatḥ al-

Bārī just this: 'He was a companion of the Prophet Muhammad ﷺ, and wrote for him. He does not provide an explicit mention which would suggest that Muʿāwiyah wrote Divine Revelation (Fatḥ al-Bārī Vol 7, p. 104). Therefore, Ibn Ḥajar's statements are consistent in al-Iṣābah as well as Fatḥ al-Bārī where he has mentioned only about 'writing' and not about 'writing Divine Revelation.'

Imam Dahabī, a highly trusted authority and a man of significant knowledge is also a medieval chronicler (d. 748 AH). He has nowhere mentioned that Muʿāwiyah wrote Divine Revelation. On the contrary, he explicitly mentions in his Islamic chronology ʿAhd Muʿāwiyah (Researched by ʿAbd al-Salām, Beirut, p. 309) and in Siyar Aʿlām al-Nubalā that: Zaid bin Thābit wrote Divine Revelation and Muʿāwiyah wrote about matters which transpired between the Prophet Muhammad ﷺ, and the Arabs.' This is exactly what has been written by the third and fourth century chronicler and secretary to the Abbasids, Muḥammad bin ʿAbdūsh al-Jahshyārī four hundred years ago.

Before him, it was the famous commentator of the Quran, traditionalist and chronicler Imam Ṭabarī who, instead of describing Muʿāwiyah as the writer of Divine Revelation, wrote thus about him: 'And Muʿāwiyah used to write about his [the Prophet Muhammad's ﷺ] requirements in his presence.' (Tārīkh, printed by Dār al-Maʿārif, Cairo Vol 6, p. 179). After Ṭabarī, it was the chronicler al-Masʿūdī (d. 347 AH) who wrote about the Prophet Muhammad's ﷺ, ten secretaries in great detail in his book al-Tanbīh wal-Ashrāf. The book recounts in detail the individual duties of the members of the secretariat who were required to write on various matters. Five secretaries have been named who, at times, used to write for the Prophet Muhammad ﷺ, temporarily. These five names contain Muʿāwiyah and it has been explicitly written thus: 'And Muʿāwiyah wrote for him ﷺ, a few months before he passed away.' (Cairo 1938, p. 246).

The references cited by the author from Ibn Ḥazm's book Jawamiʿ al-Sīrah have been done so by cutting, pasting and adding words in places the author found relevant. After narrating about Zaid bin Thābit writing Divine Revelation, he has written about Muʿāwiyah writing for the Prophet Muhammad ﷺ, but then has added the phrase, 'among other things' after Muʿāwiyah's name (Jamharah al-Tawārīkh, p. 27). We have proven through references of other medieval and early chroniclers that he wrote regarding matters that arose between the Prophet Muhammad ﷺ, and leaders of the various tribes. Among contemporary works, Dr Mustafa al-Azmi's book Kitāb al-Nabī (which contains biographies of 61 secretaries) does not mention Muāwiyah as a writer of Divine Revelation.

It is very unfortunate that those who keep on insisting that Muʿāwiyah was a writer of Divine Revelation, have chosen to remain oblivious to the fact that he accepted Islam twenty-one years after its advent on the occasion of the victory of Mecca, as we have established by way of various evidences and proofs. Therefore, a question arises as to who was writing Divine Revelation for these twenty-one years? During the revelation of the Meccan chapters and the initial eight years of revelation in Medina, was a period when Mu'awiyah was still an infidel and most of the Quran had already been documented through these years. In the last two years of the Prophet Muhammad's ﷺ, life, very little Quran was left to be revealed. Islamic history is not taught in schools where the official syllabus is followed. It is unfortunate, and extremely so, that teachers of the Ḥadith tradition do not know anything about the men who narrated those traditions and the companions who were the source of Ḥadith. I experienced this in Karachi. In Defense's two masjids, during the second sermon of the Friday prayer, I heard the name of Muʿāwiyah being taken along with the names of the Rightly Guided Caliphs. The first time, when I came out of the masjid, I told the sermonizer, 'Today, you have done grave injustice to Haẓrat Abu ʿUbaydah,

Saʿad bin Abi Waqqāṣ, Haẓrat ʿAbd al-Raḥmān bin ʿAwf and the other "foremost" companions. The imam was taken aback and said, 'Why, what happened?' I said, 'Instead of taking the names of these highly ranked companions in the second sermon, you took the name of Muʿāwiyah who accepted Islam long after it's advent.' I also asked him whether he knew when Emir Muʿāwiyah accepted Islam. He did not seem to know. When I told him that he accepted Islam merely two years before the death of the Messenger of Allah ﷺ, in year 8 AH, he went utterly silent. The second imam was a graduate of a major madrassa of Multan. He read Maulāna Ashraf ''Ali Thānwi's book in his first sermon. In his second sermon, he took the name of Muʿāwiyah along with those of the Rightly Guided caliphs. I asked him, 'Your second sermon was not of Maulāna Ashraf 'Ali Thānwi. Whose was it?' He said, 'It was a writing of Mufti Rashīd Ahmad.' Muʿāwiyah's name is not present in Maulāna Thānwi's second sermon. I asked him, 'Tell me, when did Muʿāwiyah accept Islam?' He also, like the former imam, did not know. He asked me to tell him. When I told him that Muʿāwiyah accepted Islam twenty-one years after the advent of Islam, he became uneasy. People have indulged in such an elaborate propaganda to publicize his writing of the Divine Revelation that the common populace has started to believe that he indeed was from among the foremost companions. They do not know that he was neither from among the Emigrants (Muhājirīn) and nor from among the Helpers (Anṣār) whose virtues have been recounted in the Quran and the Ḥadith.

Aurangzeb Saheb is such a passionate eulogist of Muʿāwiyah that along with describing him as a writer of Divine Revelation, he has also designated him as a 'confidant of the Prophet Muhammad'. Either this is on account of his ignorance, or it is a willfully written false statement. If he would read the Sīrah Ibn Hishām, he would know that the Prophet Muhammad's ﷺ, confidant (الـ ذ بي سر امـ ين) was Ḥaẓrat Ḥuzaifah bin al-Yamān. He was with the Prophet

Muhammad ﷺ, in the battle of Tabūk, where the Prophet Muhammad ﷺ, had told him the names of certain dissidents and advised him not to disclose those names to anyone. ‘Umar tried hard to extract those names from him but, Ḥuzaifah did not relent. It was only after the passing away of the Prophet Muhammad ﷺ, that Ḥaẓrat Ḥuzaifah told ‘Umar those names. Ḥāfiẓ Ibn Ḥajar has nicknamed him Ṣāḥib al-Sirr (Guardian of Secrets) with the references of Bukhāri and Muslim. Nobody from among the medieval chroniclers has described Muʿāwiyah as ‘Ṣāḥib al-Sirr’. How can he even be? He accepted Islam merely two years before the Prophet Muhammad’s ﷺ, death and his father had been cursed by the Prophet Muhammad ﷺ, himself on the day of the Battle of Uḥud. The Prophet Muhammad ﷺ, had said, ‘O Allah, curse Abu Sufyān.’ (Imam Dahabi, Siyar Aʿlām al-Nubalā 3/564; with reference of Imam Tirmidhī).

The teacher of Imam Aḥmed bin Ḥanbal and Imam Bukhāri, famous traditionalist Isḥāq bin Rāhweyah has explicitly stated that: ‘Anything narrated in virtue of Muʿāwiyah from the Prophet Muhammad ﷺ, is not sound’. Imam Jawzi has written the following Ḥadith in his book ‘Al ʿIlal al-Matāhiyah fi al-Aḥādīth al-Wāhiyah’ (Nashr Idārah al-ʿUlūm al-Athariyah, Faisalabad, 2nd edition, 1981): ‘O Allah, make him from among those who guide others and are themselves guided.’ An article on the same has also been written in the book Kitāb al-Faḍāil wal Manāqib, p. 274. It has been famously narrated in the Musannad of al-Imām Ḥanbal from Ḥaẓrat ʿAbdullah bin ʿAbbās who was sent by the Prophet Muhammad ﷺ, to summon Muʿāwiyah. He came to call the latter three times, and on all three occasions, he came back with the message that Muʿāwiyah was eating. Thereupon, the Prophet Muhammad ﷺ, prayed, ‘May Allah never satisfy his hunger.’ As a result, Muʿāwiyah used to eat seven times a day. His food included meat and sweetmeats, but his hunger would never cease to persist. He used to say, ‘I am tired of eating and that is why I stop, but my hunger is never satisfied.’

(Dahabī, Siyar Aʿlām al-Nubalā 3/123; and Ibn Kathīr 8)

Dahabī (Siyar Aʿlām al-Nubalā 3/143) and Ibn Kathīr (8/131) narrate on the authority of Musannad Abu Dawūd al-Ṭayālisī that ʿĀishah was asked, 'Are you not surprised that a man (Muʿāwiyah) from among the Ṭulaqā has quarrelled with the Companions as regards to the caliphate and usurped it?' She replied, 'What is there to be surprised? This is in the discretion of Allah. He bestows it upon the pious and the immoral. The Pharaohs ruled Egypt for four hundred years. Imam Dahabī has issued a verdict: 'Despite being several companions who were better than him and more capable, he ruled very intelligently with foresight and good political acumen. Yes, he indeed erred at times and he shall be judged before Allah.' (Siyar Aʿlām al-Nubalā 3/133). After writing his biography in forty-three pages, Dahabi writes in the end: 'Muʿāwiyah was among the best of rulers but he was not immune from error. May Allah forgive him.' (Siyar Aʿlām al-Nubalā 3/159).

It should be noted that Imam Dahabi has described Muʿāwiyah as the 'Best of Kings' and not a 'Caliph'. This is because it has been written in all medieval histories, and has also been narrated by Ibn Taimiyah and Ibn Khaldūn in their chronologies that Muʿāwiyah referred to himself as the 'First Among Kings' (in Islam). His methods and ways were also like kings. He used to play cards, he lived in a palace and kept servants , etc.

Regarding kingship, there is a famous Ḥadith attributed to a Companion of the Prophet Muhammad ﷺ, Safīnah, which is: 'Caliphate after me shall remain for thirty years. Then it shall become a kingdom.' (Abu Dāwūd Musannad al-Ṭayālisī). The caliphate ended immediately after Ḥasan's caliphate in 41 AH and that was when thirty years of the caliphate came to an end. According to Imam Dahabī and others, Muʿāwiyah then became the ruler and focused on lavishness and luxury. Dahabī also writes:

'If only had he not entrusted the kingdom to his son Yazīd and if only had he let the people choose their ruler for themselves' (Dahabī, 3/158).

This is the reason why Imam Ibn Ḥazm has used the word 'Caliphate' till the caliphate of Ḥasan in his book 'Asmā' al-Khulafā wal Wulāt wa Ẓikr Muddatihim' (Names of caliphs and rulers and the duration of their reigns). Meaning, he has referred to the caliphates of Abu Bakr, 'Umar, 'Uthmān, 'Ali and Ḥasan as 'caliphate' and then the duration of Muʿāwiyah's reign has been described as 'The Wilāyah (period of a king's rule) of Muʿāwiyah bin Abu Sufyān, the Wilāyah of Yazīd' and the duration of the rule of the subsequent kings has been described as Wilāyah. It is only in the case of 'Umar bin ʿAbdul ʿAzīz that the word 'Caliphate' has been used. (Jawāmiʿ al-Sīrah wa Khamsa Rasā'il Ukhrā, p. 356)

A major point of contention that refutes the claim that he wrote Divine Revelation is that the Quran was written down on paper for the first during the time of Ḥaẓrat Abu Bakr. The duty of writing down the Quran in the way it was written was entrusted to Ḥaẓrat Zaid bin Thābit by Abu Bakr. While entrusting this task to him, Abu Bakr told Zaid, 'You are an intelligent young man and have been writing Divine Revelation for a long time. Now gather all writings of the Quran and compile them into one book.' Thereupon, Zaid bin Thābit did as instructed and gathered the different pages from different sources and compiled them into one whole book in the order which we see today. Then during the time of Ḥaẓrat ʿUthmān, five or seven copies of the same Quran that was compiled by Zaid were rewritten, and that work was entrusted to Ḥaẓrat Zaid bin Thābit, ʿAbdullah bin Zubayr, Saʿīd bin al-ʿĀṣ and ʿAbd al-Raḥmān bin al-Ḥārith bin Hishām. They wrote the Quran in a single volume and used those very pages which were in the care of Ḥaẓrat Ḥafṣah. In this way, when the Quran was written two times, the task was carried out by Ḥaẓrat Zaid bin Thābit Anṣārī both times along with three Quraishi writers of Divine Revelation. If Muʿāwiyah was a writer of Divine Revelation, he would have been included in the groups wherein were included those who prepared seven copies of the Quran in a single volume during the time of Haẓrat ʿUthmān which were then sent to prominent Islamic cities. This proves that Muʿāwiyah was not among those who were the writers of Divine Revelation. Imam Suyūṭi's book on Quranic sciences 'Itqān Fann al-Qur'an' mentions this in great detail. Also worth noting is that in the Ṣaḥīḥ Bukhārī, the virtues of several Companions have been recounted under the heading of 'Manāqib'. On the other hand, Muʿāwiyah has been mentioned in a dedicated chapter titled 'Ẓikr Muʿāwiyah' which contains nothing except a jurisprudential query about the witr prayer. Ḥāfiẓ Ibn Ḥajar has commented on this Ḥadith by providing a reference of Imam Ibn al-Jawzī who narrated an extremely factual report from Imam Aḥmad about 'Ali which is as though his verdict on Emir Muʿāwiyah. He said,

"Abdullah bin Aḥmad enquired from his father Imam Aḥmad bin Ḥanbal the following: 'What do you have to say about 'Ali and Muʿāwiyah?' He lowered his head and said, 'You should know that 'Ali had many enemies meaning the Khawārij and the Nāṣibis. They tried hard to find a flaw in him but failed to do so. Therefore, they began to focus on a man who fought with him and now they sing his praises for his animosity with 'Ali.' He then summarized the gist of Imam Aḥmad's contention in the following words: 'By this he has indicated towards the fabricated virtues of Muʿāwiyah which are baseless." Then Ḥāfiẓ Ibn Ḥajar writes his own opinion in the following words: 'There are many traditions which have been narrated recounting his virtues, but prima facie, none of them are sound. The same has been said by Isḥāq bin Rāhweyah and Imam Nisā'ī, and they are steadfast in their statement.'

This is the reality of Emir Muʿāwiyah's life. Some aspects require further research and here only those aspects have been discussed which have been mentioned in the context of Maulāna Aurangzeb's misquotations and incorrect interpretations.

The common reader should remember two main points. Firstly, Muʿāwiyah accepted Islam twenty-one years after its advent that is two years before the victory of Mecca; and secondly, that he is not a writer of Divine Revelation.

THE SAYINGS OF THE GREATEST MESSENGER

OUR MASTER MUHAMMAD ﷺ

ON

MU'AWIYA THE SON OF ABI SUFYAN

HASSAN BIN 'ALI ALSAQQAF AL-HASHIMI AL-HUSAYNI

Rendered Into English

By Khusro Qasim and Sayyid Asad Amir Dean Husayni

THE SAYINGS OF THE GREATEST MESSENGER OUR MASTER MUHAMMAD ﷺ ON MU'AWIYA THE SON OF ABI SUFYAN

WHAT HAS BEEN NARRATED ABOUT MU'AWIYA FROM SLANDER IN THE SHARIAH

Many narrations authentic and good from the greatest messenger Muhammad ﷺ has been narrated in condemning Mu'awiya the son of Abi Sufyan, and the reality of Mu'awiya's actions confirm the authenticity of these blessed narrations because his actions were the opposite of the orders of Allah the almighty. Many scholars — purposely or unknowingly like Ibn Taymiyyah and his arrogant followers have attempted to refute these blessed narrations either by interpretation or weakening or rejecting these narrations. Many scholars also followed them blindly and arrogantly without investigation. Many narrations were also fabricated in the virtues of Mu'awiya by the will of Mu'awiya and his clan from his Umayyad State, so Ibn Taymiyyah and his followers raced to find chains for these narrations which were authenticated and later used as evidence[1]. While the great scholars of Hadith like An-Nas'ai, Ishaq Ibn Rahoya, Hafez Ibn Hajar and many other great Scholars

---

[1] In (Majmoo Fatawa) (35/64) and Al-Fatawa Al-Kubra (4/259), Ibn Taymiyyah mentions the Hadith: Oh Allah teach him the book (Quran) and Maths and protect him from punishment. This Hadith is fabricated which have weak men and liars in its chains. As will be later clarified.

of Ahl al-Sunnah Wal Jama'a have stated that none of the so-called virtues of Mu'awiya are authentic.

Hafez Ibn Hajar mentions in the Fateh (7/104): That Ishaq Ibn Rahoya, An-Nas'ai and Ismail the Maliki Judge said: None of the virtues of Mu'awiya are correct.

The following is what has been narrated in the authentic Prophet Muhammad's

Sunnah describing the state of Mu'awiya and the judgement upon him from the infallible Prophet Muhammad ﷺ:

1) NARRATED IN BUKHARI (447, 2812) AND MUSLIM (2916) WITH DIFFERING WORDINGS

This is the wording of Bukhari: Ammar will be killed by the rebellious (transgressing) group. He will be inviting them (i.e., his murderers, the rebellious group) to Paradise and they will invite him to Hell-fire[2] Ammar said, "I seek refuge with Allah from affliction."

Ammar Ibn Yassir was in the army of 'Ali Ibn Abi Talib, the leader of the family of the Prophet Muhammad ﷺ, fighting Mu'awiya and his group.

From this Hadith the Prophet Muhammad ﷺ concludes:

That Mu'awiya and his group are the rebellious (Transgressing) group, and the Almighty Allah has ordered us to fight rebellious (Transgressing) group as Allah states: But if one of them oppresses the other, then fight against the one that oppresses until it returns to the ordinance of Allah and that group didn't return to the order of Allah nor did its followers even till our current day.

[2] In another wording in Bukhari: Ammar will be calling to Allah and they will be calling him to Hell-fire and this Hadith has been narrated in Sahih Ibn Hiban (15/553), Ibn Abi Shaiba (6/385), Ahmed (3/90), At-Tabarani in Mujam Al-Kabeer (12/395) and many other sources. Hafez Ibn Hajar has said in Fateh Al-Bari (1/543): This Hadith Ammar will be killed by the rebellious (Transgressing) group has been narrated from a large number of Sahaba including Qatada Ibn Naman as mentioned earlier, Um Salama in Muslim, Abu Huraira in Tirmidhi, Abdullah Ibn Amr Ibn Al-Aas Ibn Al-As in An-Nasai, Uthman Ibn Affan, Hudayfa, Abu Ayub, Abu Rafa, Khuzaima Ibn Thabit, Mu'awiya, Amr Ibn Al-Aas Ibn Al-As, Abu Al Yaser, and several others companions which is too long to mention.

Say, "My Lord has only forbidden immoralities — what is apparent of them and what is concealed — and sin, and Transgression without right."

That Mu'awiya and his group are calling to hellfire

So how can we defend someone whom he and his group are callers of hell-fire?

Are we not shy from our Master Prophet Muhammad ﷺ who doesn't speak out of desire and indeed (his speech) is a revelation that is revealed?

That 'Ali and his group which have Ammar are callers to Paradise and Allah. How can we say after that: that Mu'awiya was mistaken and he had one reward and the Prophet Muhammad ﷺ says: that his group will be calling to hell-fire? Can someone calling towards hellfire have a reward?

Where are the believers that follow Allah and His Messenger ﷺ?

It is not for a believing man or a believing woman, when Allah and His Messenger have decided a matter, that they should [thereafter] have any choice about their affair. And whoever disobeys Allah and His Messenger ﷺ has certainly strayed into clear error. (Al-Ahzab: 36)

Hafez Ibn Hajar states in Fateh Albari (1/543):

This Hadith is one of the signs of the Prophecy and has a clear virtue for 'Ali and Ammar and a refutation for the Nawasib that claim that 'Ali was not right in his war.

The truth is that the person who said this is Ibn Taymiyyah Al-Hirani that some people describe as the Sheikh of Islam. Even though this title is forbidden in Islam especially for someone like him who authenticates the Hadith that Allah is in the image of the young man with a shaved beard and believes in its appearance and also says that it's a vision of the eye and not a dream.[3]

Allah Almighty is indeed Greater than this and [Glory be to your Lord, the Lord of Dominion, above what they attribute to him].

Ibn Taymiyyah says about 'Ali (May Allah be pleased with him) in Minhaj al-Sunnah (4/500 and 2/232 from another edition):

It should be said to the Rafidah: if the Nawasib told you: 'Ali permitted the blood of the Muslims and fought them without an order from Allah or His Messenger ﷺ for his political position and the Prophet Muhammad ﷺ said: (The Swearing at a Believer is transgression and his killing is disbelief) and also said: Don't return after me as disbelievers killing one another. Then 'Ali would be a disbeliever, their argument would not be stronger than yours, because the Hadiths they are using are authentic.

Also, they will say: Killing humans is corruption and whoever killed for his obedience is in indeed wanting of political position and corruption on this earth. And this is the state of Pharoah. Ibn Taymiyyah seems to have forgotten that Mu'awiya was the one who killed innocent lives without any right and as transgression. Ibn Taymiyyah doesn't apply these principles on Mu'awiya and in fact, went to the extent of comparing 'Ali to the Pharaoh and he doesn't compare Mu'awiya to that.

Indeed you should contemplate how he supported the evidence of the Nawasib that 'Ali (May Allah be pleased with him) would be a Kafir (disbeliever) according to the evidence that is more authentic in his opinion.

---

[3] That is in his book (Tasees Fi Al-Rad Ala Asas At-Taqdees) (3/241) in the handwritten edition.

The Nawasib that say these claims are indeed himself and no one else. Ibn Taymiyyah is inventing statements and attributing it to unknown people when in fact they are his sayings and beliefs.

This poor man forgot the saying of Allah the Almighty in the Quran: (Fight the Transgressors) and the narration from the Prophet Muhammad ﷺ in the authentic books about that group which will be calling to hellfire. So he narrates from his Nawasib brothers the opinion of the disbelief of 'Ali and supports them and states that their pieces of evidence are stronger.

These Nawasib that attack the major companions (May Allah be pleased with them) view that the Takfeer of 'Ali is a simple matter and just simply softly criticizing Mu'awiya is clear deviation and will claim that it is destroying the religion from its pillars.

Ibn Taymiyyah seems to have forgotten the quote of 'Ali (May Allah be pleased with him): I have been ordered to fight the Al-Naakithin (People of battle of Camel), Wal-Qasitin (Mu'awiya and his clan), and Wal-Mariqin (Khawarij) and the narration of the Prophet Muhammad ﷺ, There are of you who will fight for the interpretation of the Quran as I fought on its Revelation. Abu Bakr said: Is it me Oh Messenger ﷺ of Allah? He said: (No). 'Umar said: Is it me Oh Messenger ﷺ of Allah? He said: No, but the cleaner of the shoe. And the Prophet Muhammad ﷺ had given his shoe for 'Ali to clean. Narrated in Sahih Ibn Hiban (15/385), (Abu Ya'la) (2/341) and he authenticated it and Al-Haythami said in Al-Mijma (5/186): (Narrated by Abu Ya'la and its narrators are the narrators of Bukhari and Muslim).

And this is why the small number of companions that didn't participate in the fighting and didn't fight with 'Ali and the group which were calling to Paradise later regretted in their lives. Ibn 'Umar said:

I did not regret anything from the matter of this verse except that I didn't fight the transgressing group as Allah Almighty ordered. Narrated by Al-Hakim in Mustadrak (3/115) and it is authentic.

At-Al Dahabi in Siyar Alam An-Nubala (2/177): (There is no doubt that Aisha regretted completely her journey to Basra and her appearance at the day of the Camel ...).

Ibn Taymiyah says in Minhaj al-Sunnah (4/514):

'Ali is unable to fight the Apostates who are also disbelievers. This is very disrespectful to say such a thing, or either he is directed by arrogance.

Hafez Ibn Hajar says in Durar Al-Kamina (1/155) that Ibn Taymiyah said about 'Ali:

Some accused him of hypocrisy because of what he said about 'Ali earlier, and that he ('Ali) was disappointed as he left (the world), and he tried to take the Caliphate multiple times but was unable to, and he fought for politics not for religion, and for his saying that he was loving of position and that Uthman

loved wealth, and that Abu Bakr became Muslim as an old man knowing what he is saying whereas 'Ali converted to Islam as a boy and the Islam of a boy is not accepted in an opinion[4].

And for what he said about the engagement of the daughter of Abu Jahl and he died and didn't forget her.

And the story of Abi Al-'Aas Ibn Rabi and what was understood from it. It is these things that they accused him of.

So they accused him of hypocrisy because of the narration of the Prophet Muhammad ﷺ: No one hates you but a Hypocrite.

---

[4] See Minhaj al-Sunnah (7/155)

And when he would be judged for these things he would say I didn't mean that I meant something else. He would then mention a strange interpretation.

The Nawasib and the blind find what Ibn Taymiyyah says about 'Ali and other companions to be a simple matter but to criticize Mu'awiya in their eyes is to destroy Islam.

Ibn Hajar states in Lisan Al-Mizan (6/319-320) about Ibn Taymiyyah: How many times would he exaggerate when refuting the Rafidi which led him to devalue 'Ali (May Allah be pleased with him) sometimes.

Whereas we see Ibn Taymiyah in his books praising Mu'awiya and defending him strongly.

2) IT HAS BEEN PROVEN IN THE AUTHENTIC NARRATIONS THAT MU'AWIYA USED TO ORDER THE PEOPLE TO CURSE 'ALI (MAY ALLAH BE PLEASED WITH HIM)

And this is a great sin as according to the Shariah:

Narrated in Sahih Muslim (2404) by Amer Ibn Sa'ad Ibn Abi Waqas from his father:

Mu'awiya Ibn Abi Sufyan ordered Sa'ad (ie to swear) then he said: What prevents you from abusing Abu Turab ('Ali), whereupon he said: It is because of three things which I remember Allah's Messenger ﷺ and having said about him that I would not abuse him and even if I find one of those three things for me, it would be more dear to me than the red camels. I heard Allah's Messenger ﷺ say about 'Ali as he left him behind in one of his campaigns [that was Tabuk]. 'Ali said to him: Allah's Messenger ﷺ, you leave me behind along with women and children. Thereupon Allah's Messenger ﷺ said to him: Aren't you satisfied with being unto me what Aaron was unto Moses but with this exception that there is no Prophethood after me.

And I (also) heard him say on the Day of Khaibar: I would certainly give this standard to a person who loves Allah and His Messenger ﷺ, and Allah and His Messenger ﷺ love him too. He (the narrator) said: We had been anxiously waiting for it when he (the Holy Prophet Muhammad ﷺ) said: Call 'Ali. He was called and his eyes were inflamed. He applied saliva to his eyes and handed over the standard to him, and Allah gave him victory. (The third occasion is this) when the (following) verse was revealed: "Let us summon our children and your children." Allah's

Messenger ﷺ called 'Ali, Fatima, Hassan and Husain and said: 'O Allah, they are my family.'[5]

So contemplate on how Mu'awiya used to order the companions to swear at 'Ali (May Allah be pleased with him).

Narrated in Ibn Majah (121) with an authentic chain[6] from Sa'ad Ibn Abi Waqas:

Mu`awiya came on one of his pilgrimages and Sa`ad entered upon him. They mentioned 'Ali, and Mu'awiya abused (swore) him[7]. Sa'ad became angry and said: 'Are you saying this of a man of whom I heard the Messenger of Allah ﷺ say: "If I am a person's Mawla, 'Ali is also his Mawla." And I heard him say: "You are to me like Harun was to Musa, except that there will be no Prophet after me." And I heard him say: "I will give the banner today to a man who loves Allah and His Messenger."

This narration is clear that Mu'awiya used to abuse and swear at 'Ali.

Mu'awiya used to order his followers and leaders to swear at 'Ali and order others to do so too:

Narrated in Sahih Muslim (2409) from the companion Sahl Ibn Sa'ad:

A person from the offspring of Marwan was appointed as the governor of Medina. He called Sahl bin Sa`ad and ordered him to abuse 'Ali. Sahl refused to do that. He (the governor) said to him: If you do not agree to it (at least) say: May Allah curse Abu Turab.

[5] Narrated by Muslim (2404), Tirmidhi (3724) and others.

[6] Authenticated by Al-Albani in Sahih Ibn Majah (1/26).

[7] Which means he swore at him.

Sahl said: There was no name dearer to ‘Ali than Abu Turab (for it was given to him by the Prophet Muhammad ﷺ himself) and he felt delighted when he was called by this name.

With this said, Mu’awiya used to swear at ‘Ali (May Allah be pleased with him) and order the people to do so. It has been authentically narrated that the Prophet Muhammad ﷺ: Whosoever swears at ‘Ali has indeed sworn at me.

Narrated by Ahmed in his Musnad (6/323) with an authentic chain by

Abi Abdullah Al Jad’Ali said:

I entered upon Um Salama and she said: How is the Prophet Muhammad ﷺ being sworn at among you? I said: I seek refuge with Allah from that. She said: I heard the Messenger of Allah ﷺ say: Who so ever swears at ‘Ali has indeed sworn at me. [8]

Al-Hakim also narrated this (3/121) and added: and whoever curses me has cursed Allah.

The swearing of Mu’awiya and his clan at ‘Ali (May Allah be pleased with him) is a popular matter it is Mutawatir (successive) and requires a book on its own[9].

---

[8] Authenticated by Shuaib Al-Arnaut in his annotation of the (Musnad) (44/329) and Al-Albani Authenticated it (3332), narrated by An-Nasai in (Kubra) (5/133) and has multiple narrations as mention by Al-Haythimi in (Mijma Al-Zawaid) (9/130).

It has other wordings by other narrators; including Ibn Abi Shaiba (12/76-77), At-Tabarani in Kabir (23/322) and Abi Yala (12/444) and others.

[9] Also narrated in Musnad Ahmed (1/187), Abi Dawood (4649, 4650) and others with an authentic chain which narrates the objection of Saeed Ibn Zaid on Al-Mogeera Ibn Shu’ba that someone cursed 'Ali Ibn Abi Talib ﷺ be upon him) in his presence, Saeed Ibn Zaid said: “Oh Mogeera Ibn Shuba, can’t you hear that

So in conclusion, Mu'awiya was swearing at 'Ali and ordering others to do so too and the Prophet Muhammad ﷺ says: Who so ever swears at 'Ali has indeed sworn at me.

So are you going to be with the Prophet Muhammad ﷺ or with Mu'awiya that swore at 'Ali knowingly that whoever does so has sworn at Prophet Muhammad ﷺ.

And how can we defend someone who swears 'Ali (May Allah be pleased with him) and hence swears at the Prophet Muhammad ﷺ.

---

the companions of the Prophet Muhammad ﷺ are being sworn at in your places and you do not condemn or change it. Even Al-Albani authenticated this in Sahih Abi Dawood (3/880/3887).

Also narrated by Ibn Abi Asim (1350) from Abdulrahman Ibn Al-Baylamani said: We were with Mu'awiya and a man swore at 'Ali (May Allah be pleased with him) and swore and swore and Saeed Ibn Zaid Ibn Amr Ibn Al-Aas Ibn Nafeel said: Oh Mu'awiya 'Ali is being sworn at in your presence and you don't condemn or change. I heard the Messenger of Allah ﷺ say: You are to me like what Aaron was unto Moses.

3) THE SUPPLICATION OF THE PROPHET MUHAMMAD ﷺ: MAY ALLAH NOT FILL HIS BELLY

The Prophet Muhammad's ﷺ supplication has been accepted by Allah and he never felt full after that[10]. Even At-Al Dahabi witnessed that he would eat a lot,[11] which is why his Mu'awiya never felt full after that.

belly became deformed and was unable to give sermons except by sitting down. He was also the first to give sermons while sitting in Islam[12].

Narrated in Sahih Muslim (2604) from Ibn Abbas (May Allah be pleased with him) that the Prophet Muhammad ﷺ said to him:

Go and call Mu'awiya. I returned and said, he is busy in taking food. He again asked me to go and call Mu'awiya to him. I went (and came back) and said that he was busy in taking food, whereupon he said, "May Allah not fill his belly."

Imam An-Nas'ai, the author of the Sunan, was killed because of this matter in the Sham. At-Al Dahabi mentions in Tathkerat Al-Hufad (2/699) that An- Nas'ai said:

---

[10] At-Al Dahabi says in Siyar Alam An-Nubala (3/123): That Al-Hakim added that

[11] At-Al Dahabi says in Siyar Alam An-Nubala[(3/124): That Mu'awiya was considered from the big eaters.

[12] Narrated by Ibn Abi Shaiba in his (Musanaf) (7/237), Ahad walMuthani) (1/380), Fateh Al-Bari (2/401), and Siyar Alam An-Nubala (13/485) that the Prophet Muhammad's ﷺ Sunnah is to give sermons while standing.

I entered Damascus and the haters of ‘Ali were many so I created the book of Virtues of ‘Ali so maybe Allah may guide them[13].

Al Dahabi says in Siyar Alam An-Nubala (14/132): An-Nas’ai left Egypt at the end of his life towards Damascus, where he was asked about Mu’awiya and what has been narrated about his virtues, so he said: Does he not accept that we are not even mentioning him (i.e. his negatives) So they continued beating him up till they removed him from the mosque. Al-Daraqutni said: He left to go to Hajj and was trialled in Damascus and achieved martyrdom.

At-Al Dahabi says in Siyar Alam An-Nubala (14:129-130):

This is also a refutation to those who reject or interpret the Hadith (Oh Allah never fill his belly) and use the Hadith (Oh Allah whomsoever I cursed or swore at making it reward and mercy for him) therefore it becomes a virtue.

Furthermore, the interpretation of the Prophet Muhammad’s ﷺ saying: (Oh Allah never fill his belly) as in Sahih Muslim (2604) that it’s a virtue because of the Hadith: (Oh Allah whomsoever I cursed or swore at make it a reward and mercy for him) is a false interpretation for two main reasons:

Firstly, At-Al Dahabi admits that Mu’awiya was from the big eaters. Hence the Prophet Muhammad’s ﷺ supplication was

---

[13] See (Tahtheeb Al-Kamal) (1/338) for Al-Mizi, (Tahtheeb At-Tahtheeb) (1/33) for Hafez Ibn Hajar and (Kashef Al-Dunoon) (1/706).

They told him (i.e., An-Nas’ai): Why don’t you narrate the virtues of Mu'awiya. He said: what should I narrate: Oh Allah never fill his belly. So the questioner didn’t i.e. respond.

At-Al Dahabi says about Mu'awiya: That Mu’awiya was considered from the big eaters.

This is an important confession from him because At-Al Dahabi admits that the Prophet Muhammad’s ﷺ supplication was accepted.

accepted. That is why he was unable to deliver sermons except by sitting which proves the Prophet Muhammad's ﷺ supplication was accepted[14] This is clear slander for Mu'awiya.

Secondly, the Hadith is specific, not general. Muslim narrated (2603) from Anas Ibn Malik: (So for any person from amongst my Ummah whom I curse and he in no way deserves it, let that, O Lord, be made a source of purification and purity and nearness to (Allah) on the Day of Resurrection).

---

[14] As in Siyar Alam al Nubala (3/156-157), Fateh Al-Bari (2/401), (Musanaf Ibn Abi Shaiba) (7/247), (Al-Ahad Wal-Muthani) (1/380) and also narrated By Al-Khateeb in (Modeh Owham Al-Jama Wal-Tafreeq) (1/348) from Jaber Ibn Samora said: I saw the Prophet Muhammad ﷺ give sermons standing and whosoever says otherwise is a liar. This proves that Mu'awiya or his clan used to claim that the Prophet Muhammad ﷺ used to give sermons while sitting to justify for Mu'awiya sitting in the sermons.

Furthermore, the addition of the statement (and he in no way deserves it) in this narration, makes this interpretation very weak. As known in the science of Usool, that if the evidence is not clear it cannot be used as evidence.

4) IMAM AHMED IBN HANBAL NARRATES MU'AWIYA USED TO DRINK ALCOHOL IN HIS CALIPHATE

Allah says: Indeed, intoxicants, gambling, [sacrificing on] stone alters [to other than Allah, and divining arrows are but defilement from the work of Satan, so avoid it that you may be successful and the Prophet Muhammad ﷺ said: When an adulterer commits illegal sexual intercourse, then he is not a believer at the time, he is doing it, and when a drinker of an alcoholic liquor drinks it, then he is not a believer at the time of drinking it (Bukhari 2475).

The narrations in the condemning of the drinker of alcohol are many and popular and its prohibition is very well known.

Narrated by Ahmed Ibn Hanbal in his Musnad (5/347) from Abdullah Ibn Burayda said: I and my father entered Upon Mu'awiya and then he sat us down on the mats, then we were served with food and we all ate. Then we were served with drinks and (only) Mu'awiya drank and then he served my father and said: I haven't consumed this since the Prophet Muhammad ﷺ forbid it.[15]

Hafez Al-Haythimi in (Mijma Alzawaid) (5/42) said: (Its men are the narrators of Bukhari and Muslim).

Mu'awiya also had caravans of alcohol which he would sell. At-Al Dahabi narrates in (Siyar Alam An-Nubala) (2/9-10) a story of Mu'awiya selling Alcohol:

---

[15] Shuaib Al-Arnaout in his annotation on (Siyar Alam An-Nubala) (5/52) said its chain is good and the narration is in (Tareekh Dimashq) (27/127) by Ibn Asaker.

Yahya Ibn Salim from Ibn Khuthaym from Ismail Ibn Abaid Ibn Rafa from his father: That Obada Ibn Al-Samit was in AlSham and a caravan of alcohol went passed him, he said: What is this? Is it Oil? They said: No it is Alcohol being sold for X[16]. So he took a blade from the market place and destroyed every container. Abu Huraira at the time was in Alsham, so X sent for Abu Huraira and said: Can you please stop your brother Obada Ibn Alsamit?

In the day he goes to the market place and corrupts the dhimmi businesses, and in the night he sits in the Masjid doing nothing but swearing at us and calling out our mistakes. So Abu Huraira went to Obada: Oh Obada, please leave Mu'awiya and whatever he wants to sell[17]. He said: You were not with us when we pledged Allegiance that we will listen and obey and enjoy the good and forbid the evil and not fear anyone but Allah, Abu Huraira remain silent. Then X sent a letter to Uthman that Obada has corrupted Al-Sham on me[18][19].

Obada also objected against many forbidden things Mu'awiya used to do including his dealing with interest as authentically narrated in Sahih Muslim (1587) and Sunan An-Nas'ai (7/275 or 4562).

---

[16] X is Mu'awiya as is exposed later in the narration. Usually, if they want to cover someone's mistakes or crimes that will replace the name with X or a manAl-Arnaout, so they cover up for him.

[17] This statement exposes who is meant by X, so contemplate and stop the defending of the criminals.

[18] Poor man, Obada didn't leave him to sell alcohol and corrupted his business.

[19] This story is narrated by Ibn Asaker in Tareek Dimashq (7/211) and Shuaib Al-Arnaout said in his annotation on Siyar Alam An-Nubala (2/10): Its chain can be good. I say: This is good that Sheikh Shuaib said this and great thanks to him.

Mu'awiya was not the only one who used to trade with alcohol. Many of his clan and leaders were also trading with alcohol at the time of 'Umar's Caliphate (May Allah be pleased with him). It has been authentically narrated that 'Umar Ibn Al-Khattab (May Allah be pleased with him) cursed Samura because he was the first to sell alcohol (Samura was from Mu'awiya's clan and top leaders):

Narrated by Sahih Muslim (1582) from Ibn Abbas that he said: This news reached 'Umar that Samura had sold wine, whereupon he said: May Allah destroy Samura; does he not know that Allah's Messenger ﷺ said: "Let there be the curse of Allah upon the Jews that fat was declared forbidden for them, but they melted it and then sold it."

It is also narrated in Bukhari (2223) however it has been replaced with X instead of Samura's name to cover up on his crime.

It has also been narrated in the Sunan of Saeed Ibn Mansour (819) with a good chain from Ibn 'Umar: 'Umar Ibn Al-Khattab (May Allah be pleased with him) said: May Allah curse X he was the first to sell Alcohol[20], the selling of it is not permitted except for the one who it is permitted to eat or drink it.

Of course, 'Umar Ibn Al-Khattab (May Allah be pleased with him) did not say X, he mentioned his name, but the narrators covered up his name fearing Mu'awiya and Bani Ummayah or it could be simply because they want to cover up for him. It is clear also that the X is referring to Samura because in the Musnad of 'Umar Ibn Al-Khattab by Yaqoub Ibn Shaiba (1/47) from Taoous said: (The news reached 'Umar that Samura had sold alcohol).[21]

---

[20] Narrated by Ibn Abi Shaiba (7/271).

[21] As previously mentioned narrated in Sahih Muslim (1582) with Samura's name and in Bukhari (2223) without his name as usual.

Also, the servant of the family of Mu'awiya was Wahshi Ibn Harb who would not leave alcohol even after entering Islam and until the time of Mu'awiya in Sham:

Hafez Ibn Hajar says in (Tahtheeb At-Tahtheeb) (11/99) about Wahshi:

He lived in Hems and was addicted to alcohol. 'Umar used to give him two thousand then reduced it to three hundred because of alcohol addiction.

Hafez Ibn Hajar said in (Fateh Al-Bari) (7/368):

In a narration from AbdulRahman Ibn Yazid Ibn Jabir: I left with UbaidUllah Ibn Adi in a conquest in summer at the time of Mu'awiya, and we stopped by Hums on our journey.

He said (Can we meet Wahshi) Ibn Harb the servant of Jaber Ibn Mutam.

He said (Ask him about the killing of Hamza) in the narration of AlKashmeheni and ask him about the killing of Hamza, Ibn Ishaq added: and how he killed him.

He said, We asked about him and they said in the narration of Ibn Ishaq,[22] A man said to us that he was intoxicated with alcohol so if you find him awake he may speak Arabic so ask him or if not then leave him. In the Tayalosi [23] narration: if you find him intoxicated with alcohol don't ask him. This is very clear that Wahshi, the killer of Hamza, was addicted to alcohol even after his Islam.

---

[22] It is an authentic narration by Ibn Ishaq narrating in (Sunan Al-Kubra) by Al-Bayhaqi (9/97). It is also mentioned by At-Al Dahabi in (Siyar Alam An-Nubala) (1/174).

[23] Narrated by Al-Tayalosi (Page 186) with an authentic chain with the same chain as Bukhari. Also narrated in (Sunan Al-Kubra) by Al-Bayhaqi (9/97) and Bukhari's narration doesn't have that Wahashi was addicted to alcohol.

5) OBADA IBN AL-SAMIT SAYS THAT MU'AWIYA ORDERS HIM WITH WHAT IS REJECTED AND UTHMAN IBN AFFAN ACKNOWLEDGES THAT

In Mustadrak Al-Hakim (3/357) from Ubaid Ibn Rafah:

Obada Ibn Al-Samit stood up one time in the house of Uthman Ibn Affan (May Allah be pleased with him); and said: I heard the Messenger of Allah ﷺ say:

After me will be leaders who will enjoin you with what you reject, and forbid you with what you accept, so there is no obedience to whoever disobeys Allah. By Allah, Mu'awiya is one of those and Uthman didn't reply anything[24] I say: This proves that Uthman Ibn Affan accepts the slander of Mu'awiya by Obada.

---

[24] Authentic. The Hafez Sayid Ahmed Ibn As-Sidiq Al-Gumari Al-Hasani in (Al- Madawi) (4/251): [Al-Bayhaqi] The Hadith is correct and At-Al Dahabi used Tadlees as an excuse as he said Abdullah Ibn Waqid narrated this only himself however Abdullah the mentioned is not the only narrator. In Mustadrak itself, after two chains that Al-Hakim authenticates and At-Al Dahabi agrees, but At-Al Dahabi needs to claim that Abdullah Ibn Waqid is the only narrator because the Hadith is condemning Mu'awiya and Bani Ummayah. At-Al Dahabi cannot handle to hear a slander on Bani Ummayah and Mu'awiya but he may be fine to hear that on the family of the Prophet Muhammad ﷺ and 'Ali and blessings be upon them).

6) HADITH: THE FIRST TO CHANGE MY SUNNAH IS SOMEONE FROM BANI UMMAYAD AUTHENTIC [Al-Albani in his Sahih:(4/329 or 1749)]

Also, it is narrated by Ibn Abi Shaiba (7/260) from Abi Thar, and by Ibn Adi in (Al-Kamel) (3/164) narrated in the wording: The matter of my Ummah will be ruled by justice until a man takes over from Bani Ummayad[25].

[25] This Hadith is good. Narrated by Al-Bazar (4/109) from Abi Obeida, Al-Harith Ibn Abi Usama (2/642), Abu Yala (2/175-176), and Nuaim Ibn Hamad in Fitan (1/280- 282). Hafez Al-Haythami said in Mijma Al-Zawaid (5/241): Narrated by Abu Yala and AlBazar and the men in Abu Yala are the men of Bukhari and Muslim except that Mukhool never met Aba Obeida.

7) A CLEAR AUTHENTIC NARRATION THAT MU'AWIYA WILL NOT DIE ON THE RELIGION OF ISLAM

It has been narrated with an authentic chain by Al-Baladuri (d.270H) in Tareekh Al-Kabeer:

Narrated by Ishaq from 'Abd al-Razzaq from Ma'mar from Ibn Taoous from his father that Abdullah Ibn Amr Ibn Al-Aas Ibn Al-A's said: I was sitting with the Prophet Muhammad ﷺ and then he said: The next person to be entering from here when he dies he will not die on my religion. I said: I had left my father outside dressing and I was scared it was him. Then Mu'awiya entered.

The chain is authentic.

The Hafez Sayid Ahmed Ibn As-Siddiq Al-Ghumari said in Junat Al-Attar (2/154):

This Hadith is authentic based on the men of Muslim. It removes any doubt for any confused believer about this tyrant and destroys any argument that may

In Tareekh Qazween for Al-Rafaei (1/475) from Hisham Ibn Ourwa from his father from Jabir from Abu Obeida. Al-Manawi in Fayd Al-Qadeer (3/94 or 2841) that it was also narrated by Al-Rowyani and Ibn Asaker. The Sayed Hajez Ahmed Ibn As-Sadiq Al-Gumari in Al-Madawi said that Al-Dolabi narrated it in Al-Kuna (1/163) from Abu Thar.

Strangely you will hear that many of the narrators have this Hadith in their books but they say: X entered and don't mention the name of Mu'awiya to cover up for him and their ways of Nasb and hatred of the family of the Prophet Muhammad ﷺ and blessings be upon them). So praise to Allah for protecting this religion regardless of the distortions they may attempt.

In Mijma Al-Zawaid (5/243), it mentions the Hadith in At-Tabarani with (a man entered) like that wording.

Furthermore, supporting this Hadith is the Hadith narrated by Al-Bazar in his Musnad (6/46) by the companion Al-Miqdad Ibn Al-Aswad (May Allah be pleased with him) said:

By Allah, we do not guarantee anybody paradise until we know on what belief they died especially after the Hadith I heard from the Prophet Muhammad ﷺ says: The heart of the son of Adam is more changing than destiny.

Al-Bazar said after the Hadith: The correct for me is that it's (the saying of) Miqdad and its chain is good.[26]

The companions are from the sons of Adam and they are not infallible unlike the Prophet Muhammad's ﷺ and blessings be upon them) which are infallible.

[26] It is narrated by At-Tabarani in Mujam Al-Kabeer (20/252). The Wahabi Salafi Hamdi said in the annotation of this Hadith: Our sheikh said in the Silsila As-Saheeha (2/703): This isnad (chain) is authentic based on Muslim's conditions.

8) MU'AWIYA'S KILLING OF THE GREAT COMPANION HIJR IBN ADI (MAY ALLAH BE PLEASED WITH HIM) BY EXECUTION BECAUSE HE OBJECTED TO THE SWEARING OF 'ALI AND HIS KILLING FOR ABDULRAHMAN IBN UDAIS WHICH IS ONE OF THE PEOPLE OF THE TREE

At-Al Dahabi said in Siyar Alam An-Nubala (3/466) about Hijr Ibn Adi Ibn Awon said from Muhammad Ibn Sireen said: when Hijr was brought he said bury me in my clothes as I will be resurrected as angry[27]. Ibn Awon narrates from Nafe I said:

Ibn 'Umar was shopping when the news of the killing of Hijr arrived and he was overtaken by weeping. Narrated by Hisham Ibn Hassan Albakr from Muhammad: When Hijr was brought forward to Mu'awiya he said: Asalaam 'Alaikum oh Leader of the Believers. He said: Am I really the leader of the Believers? Kill him. He then prayed two units of Salah then said to his family, don't remove any of the chains nor wash any of my blood because I will be challenging Mu'awiya at a great place[28]. Hafez Ibn Hajar said in Isab (1/315): He was killed in Marj Athra from an order by

[27] Narrated in Ibn Abi Shaiba (6/446) with an authentic chain.

[28] Narrated by Al-Hakim in Mustadrak (3/469) and narrated by several companions (May Allah be pleased with them) who fought with 'Ali like Ammar Ibn Yasir and Zaid bin Sahwan that they said, Don't wash my clothes or wash my blood as I will meet in the day of judgment like this, as can be found in Talkhees Al-Habeer (2/144), Tabaqat Ibn Sa'ad (3/262), Tareekh Baghdad (8/439), Musanaf Abd al- Razzaq (3/542), Tareekh Al-Bukhari (3/397), Tamheed for Ibn 'Abd al-Barr (24/245-246), Sunan Al-Bayhaqi (8/186) and many others.

Mu'awiya[29], and Hijr was the one who conquested it and was destined to die in it. Ibn Hajar had said before that:

Hijr Ibn Adi witnessed Qadisiya and after that battle of the Camel, Siffin and was one of the leaders of 'Ali. Al-Bukhari (3/72) and Ibn Abi Hatim (3/266) both said: He was killed during the time of Aisha (May Allah be pleased with her).

Some of the arrogant people who Allah has blinded say that it doesn't hurt Mu'awiya that he killed Hijr and other of the companions because he was doing it as Ijtihad (interpretation). This opinion is weak and against the clear evidence of the Quran and the Prophet Muhammad ﷺ and blessing be upon him) saying: The killer of Ammar is in Hell-Fire[30] and against the saying in Bukhari (447) that Ammar will be killed by the rebellious (transgressing) group. He will be inviting them (i.e., his murderers, the rebellious group) to Paradise and they will invite him to Hell-fire.

The Wahabis deny that Hijr was a companion based on claims of some of the contemporary scholars which is not based on evidence. Many great scholars of Ahl al-Sunnah Wal Jama'a have stated that he is a companion including:

Al-Hakim said in Mustadrak (3/479): The mentioning of the virtues and death of Hijr Ibn Adi which was known as the young Rahib of the companions of Muhammad ﷺ and blessing be upon him).

---

[29] Ibn Sireen said Hijr was killed by an order of Mu'awiya as in Musanaf 'Abd al- Razzaq (3/242), (5/273) and its chain is authentic.

[30] It is an authentic narration narrated by Ahmed (4/372) and Ibn Sa'ad in Tabaqat (3/260) and authenticated by Al-Albani in his Sahih (5/18/2008).

At-Al Dahabi said in Siyar Alam An-Nubala (3/463):

Hijr Ibn Adi, the father of Abdul-Rahman, the Martyr, he has companionship and a rival to the Prophet Muhammad ﷺ.

Some will attempt to deny that he is a companion to attempt to decrease the severity of the crime. For the sake of argument let us assume he is not a companion, is he not a believer and a pious person? Allah says: But whoever kills a believer intentionally, his recompense is Hell, wherein he will abide eternally, and Allah has become angry with him and has cursed him and has prepared for him a great punishment. (Al-Nisa: 93)

Ibn Kathir mentions in Bidaya Wal Nihaya (6/226):

Yaqoub Ibn Sufyan said: from Ibn Baker, from Ibn Lohay'a, from Al-Harith, from Yazid, from Abdullah Ibn Zarir Al-Gafaqi said: I heard 'Ali Ibn Abi Talib say: Oh people of Iraq, seven of you will be killed in Athra like the people of Akhdood.[31]

This is very good from someone like him to not claim it's fabricated or severely weak.

So Hijr Ibn Adi and his supporters were killed.

Al-Bayhaqi said: 'Ali will not know such information except that he heard it from the Prophet Muhammad ﷺ and blessing be upon him and his family).

[31] Also narrated by Aisha, the mother of the believers: Some People will be killed in Athra whom Allah and the heavens will be angered by. Narrated from Yaqoob Ibn Sufyan by Ibn Asaker in Tareek Dimashq (12/226) and the chain has a gap. However, the story is very popular and even Al-Albani narrated Aisha's narration in his weak complication (3723) and classified as weak.

9) THE KILLING OF ABDULRAHMAN IBN UDAIS ALBALAWI FROM THE PEOPLE OF THE ALLEGIANCE OF RIDWAN PRAISED

He is one of the companions that Mu'awiya killed. At-Al Dahabi said in Tareekh Al-Islam (3/531): He has companionship and gave allegiance under the tree and has narrations. He was one of those who rebelled against Uthman and went with those to fight him[32], and then Mu'awiya managed to get hold of him and prisoned him with a group of others. He managed to escape however was recaptured in the mountains of Lebanon and was killed. Before he was executed, he told his capturers: Woe to you. Fear Allah in my blood as I am from the people of the tree, they said: The trees in the mountain are many and then killed him.

[32] Mu'awiya rebelled against 'Ali and set forth his fighting.

10) IN SAHIH BUKHARI MU'AWIYA SAYS THAT HE AND HIS SON (THE FASIQ) ARE MORE WORTHY OF THE CALIPHATE THAN UMAR IBN Al-Khattab AND HIS SON ABDULLAH. MU'AWIYA BELIEVES THAT HIS FASIQ SON IS MORE WORTHY THAN UMAR IBN Al-Khattab AND HIS SON FOR THE CALIPHATE

Narrated in Sahih Bukhari (4108) that Ibn 'Umar said: I went to Hafsa and said, "The condition of the people is as you see, and no authority has been given to me. Hafsa said, (to me), 'Go to them, and as they (i.e., the people) are waiting for you, and I am afraid your absence from them will produce division amongst them." So Hafsa did not leave Ibn 'Umar till we went to them. When the people differed, Mu'awiya addressed the people saying,

"If anybody wants to say anything in this matter of the Caliphate, he should show up and not conceal himself, for we are more rightful to be a Caliph than he and his father." On that, Habib bin Masalama said to Ibn 'Umar, "Why don't you reply to him (i.e., Mu'awiya)? Abdullah bin 'Umar said, "I untied my garment that was going around my back and legs while I was sitting and was about to say, 'He who fought against you and your father for the sake of Islam is more rightful to be a Caliph, but I was afraid that my statement might produce differences amongst the people and cause bloodshed[33], and my statement might be interpreted not as I intended. So I kept quiet remembering what Allah has prepared in

---

[33] Contemplate on how the companions are fearful when opposing Mu'awiya that their blood may be shed. Contemplate Oh those defending this tyrant. This is for those who claim that how can the companions have stayed quiet if Mu'awiya was oppressing so much.

the Gardens of Paradise for those who are patient and prefer the Hereafter to this worldly life. Habib said, "You did what kept you safe and secure (i.e., you were wise in doing so)."

Mu'awiya clearly in this narration says that he and his son are better than the second rightly guided Caliph and more worthy than him and his son Abdullah Ibn 'Umar.

Ibn Taymiyyah says in Minhaj al-Sunnah (7/453):

There were none of the kings better than Mu'awiya as he is the best of the kings of Islam and his biography is the best of any king after him.

We will further see how Mu'awiya and his actions from killing companions and innocent people, drinking alcohol, swearing at 'Ali and ordering people to do so, taking people's wealth in falsehood by the testimony of companions and enjoying the evil according to Obada and the acceptance of Uthman (May Allah be pleased with him). All this and Ibn Taymiyah Al-Hirani believes he has a good biography.

Like this, they manage to flip the falsehood into truth.

11) ONE OF THE TAB'EEN SAYS TO ABDULLAH IBN AMR IBN AL-AAS IBN AL A'S THAT MU'AWIYA IS ORDERING US TO PUT OUR WEALTH INTO FALSEHOOD AND KILL OURSELVES. IBNAMR IS UNABLE TO DENY THIS CLAIM ON MU'AWIYA

Narrated by Sahih Muslim (1844) and others from Abdul-Rahman Ibn Abd-Rab Al-Kaba said to Abdullah Ibn Amr Ibn Al-Aas bin al-As This cousin of yours, Mu'awiya, orders us to unjustly consume our wealth among ourselves and to kill ourselves, while Allah says: "O ye who believe, do not consume your wealth among yourselves unjustly, unless it is trade based on mutual agreement, and do not kill yourselves. Verily, God is Merciful to you."

The narrator says that (hearing this) Abdullah bin 'Amr Ibn Al-Aas bin al-As kept quiet for a while and then said: Obey him in so far as he is obedient to God and disobey him in matters involving disobedience to God.

12) MU'AWIYA ATTEMPTING TO REJECT NARRATIONS FORBIDDING INTEREST BASED ON THE FACT HE DID NOT HEAR IT FROM THE PROPHET MUHAMMAD ﷺ

Narrated by Sahih Muslim (1587) and in An-Nas'ai in his Sunan (7/275 or 4562) and the wording is for Sahih Muslim from Muslim Ibn Yasar and Abdullah Ibn UbadiUllah they said:

Obada said: I heard Allah's Messenger ﷺ forbidding the sale of gold by gold, and silver by silver, and wheat by wheat, and barley by barley, and dates by dates, and salt by salt, except like for like and equal for equal. So he who made an addition or who accepted an addition (sinned) interest. So the people returned what they had got.

This reached Mu'awiya and he stood up to deliver an address. He said: What is the matter with people that they narrate from the Messenger ﷺ, such tradition which we did not hear though we saw him (the Holy Prophet Muhammad ﷺ) and lived in his company.

Thereupon, Obada ibn Al Samit stood up and repeated that narration, and then said: We will narrate what we heard from Allah's Messenger ﷺ, though it may be unpleasant to Mu'awiya (or he said: even if it is against his will).

This is authenticated by Al-Albani in Sahih An-Nas'ai (3/946). The narration that gold can't be sold except for gold at the same weight is narrated by several companions, not Obada Ibn Al-Samit alone. Even if he was the only narrator it should be enough of an evidence to forbid interest. Other companions who narrate this include 'Umar Ibn Al-Khattab (Bukhari 2134), Abi Bakra (Bukhari 2175), Abi Sa'eed Al-Kudri (Bukhari 2177) and others.

This Hadith proves that Mu'awiya used to deal with interest.

Al-Qurtubi said in his Tafseer (7/392) from Imam Malik that Mu'awiya used to deal with Interest: Narrated from Ibn Wahb from Malik that he said: The land that evil is being practised should not be lived in, and the evidence for this is the action of Abi Ad-Darda when he left the land of Mu'awiya when he was dealing with interest as he allowed gold to be sold more than its weight. This is narrated in authentic books.

13) MU'AWIYA IS WEARING GOLD, SILK AND SITTING ON BEAST SKIN BY THE WITNESS OF A COMPANION AND THE ISLAM FORBIDS THIS

Even At-Al Dahabi admits that Mu'awiya was not innocent of wrong and here are some of these narrations with authentic chains. At-Al Dahabi says in Siyar Alam An-Nubala (3/158):

Al-Miqdam Ibn Ma'dikarib and a man of Banu Asad from the people of Qinnisrin went to Mu'awiya Ibn Abu Sufyan. Mu'awiya said to al-Miqdam: Do you know that Al-Hasan Ibn 'Ali has died? Al-Miqdam recited the Qur'anic verse "We belong to Allah and to Him we shall return."[34]

He (Mu'awiya) asked him: Do you think it is a calamity? He replied: Why should I not consider it a calamity when it is a fact that the Messenger of Allah ﷺ used to take him on his lap, saying: This belongs to me and Husayn belongs to 'Ali?

The man of Banu Asad said: (He was) a live coal which Allah has extinguished. Al-Miqdam said:[35] I adjure you by Allah; did you hear the Messenger of Allah ﷺ forbidding us to wear gold, prohibited the wearing of silk, and prohibited the wearing of the skins of beasts of prey and riding on them?

Mu'awiya said: Yes.

---

[34] In the narration of Abi Dawood (4131): Al-Miqdam returned i.e. recited the Qur'anic verse "We belong to Allah and to Him we shall return."

[35] In the narration of Abi Dawood (4131): Today I shall continue to make you angry and make you hear what you dislike.

Al-Miqdam said: I swear by Allah, I saw all this in your house, O Mu'awiya. Mu'awiya said: I know that I cannot be saved from you, O Miqdam.[36]

At-Al Dahabi says after this narration: Its chain is strong. Mu'awiya is one of the best kings whose justice was more than their oppression[37] and he is not innocent of wrong and Allah will forgive him. End quote from At-Al Dahabi in Siyar.

So contemplate of how they are defending the falsehood and Mu'awiya is admitting he is doing wrong.

This Hadith is clear that he is disobeying the Sunnah of the Prophet Muhammad ﷺ in front of other companions.

The annotator in Siyar Al-Nubala accepts that the narrator Baqiya said who the speaker was in another narration.

---

[36] Narrated by Abi Dawood (4131), At-Tabarani in Kabeer (20/269), and by Ahmed (4/132) but to an extent where the deviancy of Mu'awiya can't be revealed. It was revealed in Ahmed's narration that the speaker was Mu'awiya. Al-Albani classified the Hadith as authentic in Sahih Abi Dawood (2/778). Also narrated in An-Nasai in short (4255). The commentator in Siyar accepts that the narrator Baqiya said who the speaker was in another narration.

[37] No proof for this the opposite is correct.

14) IBN ABBAS AND SAMURA CURSE MU'AWIYA AND AISHA CURSES AMR Ibn Al-Aas BIN AL-AS UMAR IBN AL KHATTAB CURSES SAMURA THE FRIEND OF MU'AWIYA

Narrated by Al-Hakim in Mustadrak (4/13) from Aisha (May Allah be pleased with her): May Allah curse Amr Ibn Al-Aas Ibn Al-'As Amr Ibn Al-Aas had been one of the supporters and leaders of Mu'awiya in his wars.

In Musnad Ahmed (1/217) with an authentic chain that Ibn Abbas cursed Mu'awiya however in this narration Mu'awiya's name was replaced by X to cover up for him.

Ibn Abbas said: May Allah curse X, they destroyed the decoration of the days of Hajj. Indeed the decoration of Hajj is the Talbiya chanting.

The narration in Sahih Ibn Khuzaima (4/260) proves that X is referring to Mu'awiya: Sa'eed Ibn Jubair said: We were with Ibn Abbas in Arafah and he said: Oh Sa'eed why are the people not doing Talbiya (chanting) I said: they are scared of Mu'awiya.[38]

He said: So Ibn Abbas got up and said: Labayk Allahuma Allahuma Labayk... They have left the Sunnah from the hatred of 'Ali[39].

---

[38] This proves Mu'awiya used to enjoy the evil and forbid the good and none of the Muslims or companions can object.

[39] This narration is authentic. Narrated by Al-Hakim in Mustadrak (1/464-465) and authenticated by him. An-Nasai narrated it in Sunan Al-Kubra (2/419) and Sugra (5/253) and authenticated by Al-Albani in Sahih An-Nasai (2/631 or 2812). Also narrated in Aldeya Fi AlMuktara (10/378).

Ibn Kathir mentions in Bidaya from Jafar bin Sulaiman Ad-Dabi said: Mu'awiya appointed Samura for six months then removed him. Samura said: May Allah curse Mu'awiya if I had been obedient to Allah like I am obedient to Mu'awiya he would never punish me[40].

Ibn Abi Shaiba (2/108) narrates with an authentic chain that 'Ali ﷺ be upon him) used to say in his nightly supplications:

Oh Allah fights Mu'awiya and his clan, Amr Ibn Al-Aas Ibn Al-'As and his clan, Aba Al-Awar As-Sulami and his clan and Abdullah Ibn Qais and his clan.

Narrated in Baladhuri with an authentic chain in Ansab Al-Ashraf (2/75) with the wording as follows: 'Ali said: Oh Allah curse 6Mu'awiya the son of Abi Sufyan firstly, Amr Ibn Al-Aas Ibn Al As secondly, Aba Al-Awar As-Sulami thirdly and Abdullah Ibn Qais fourthly.

Concerning the narration in Bukhari (3765) from Ibn Abbas when asked about Mu'awiya he said he is a Faqih (i.e., a learned man who can give religious verdicts), this is from the alterations of the narrators. At-Tahawai in Sharh Ma'nee Al-Athar (1/289) narrated the same story as Mu'awiya got up and prayed one unit as Witr then Ibn Abbas said: Where did the donkey get that from? Its chain is authentic.

The Sheikh Al-Kawthari (May Allah be pleased with him) said that Ibn Abbas said he was a Faqih out of fear from Mu'awiya. Regardless the authentic narration is that he called him Donkey, not Faqih as in two chains of narrations.

---

[40] See Tareekh At-Tabari (3/240), Bidaya Wal Nihaya (8/67), Al-Kamil Fi Tareekh Ibn Athir (3/343) and (7/275).

Sheikh Al-Kawthari mentions in his Al-Nukat Fi Altahdeeth An Rodood Ibn Abi Shaibe Ala Aba Hanifa (Page 186) from the chapter of (Witr with one unit of prayer):

If it was correct that Ibn Abbas said Faqih then it was out of fear because Ibn Abbas fought under the banner of 'Ali (May Allah be pleased of him) so he needed to be careful when speaking in public gatherings.

It has also been narrated that Mu'awiya was the first to sit in the sermons and the rest of Banu Ummayah continued upon this as in Al-Kamil for Ibn Athir (4/555). Likewise, Mu'awiya was the first to stop doing takbeer in the prayers as mentioned in Fateh(2/270).

In Musnad Ahmed (4/195), Sahih Ibn Hiban (7/216) and other sources that the companion Sharhabeel Ibn Hasana (May Allah be pleased with him) used to say: I companioned the Prophet Muhammad ﷺ and Amr Ibn Al-Aas was more deviated than his donkey.

15) THE MESSENGER CURSES ALHAKAM AND HIS OFFSPRING WHICH INCLUDES MARWAN IBN ALHAKAM ONE OF THE GREATEST SUPPORTERS OF MU'AWIYA IN HIS ACTIONS

Hafez Al-Haythami in Mijma Al-Zawaid (5/241):

Shaibi said: I heard Abdullah Ibn Zubair say as he was resting on the Kabaa:

By the Lord of this Kabaa that the Prophet Muhammad ﷺ cursed X and his offspring[41]. Narrated by Ahmed and Bazar which said: Allah has cursed Al-Hakam and his offspring on the tongue of the Prophet Muhammad[42] ﷺ. At-Tabarani narrated it like this and the men of Ahmed are the Men of Bukhari and Muslim.

Al-Manawi says in Feydh Al-Qadeer (6/355):

Al-Qurtubi said: It is fearless the actions of Bani Ummayah from spilling of blood to stealing of the wealth and destroying the people in the Arabian Peninsula and Iraq and other places. He said: The majority of Bani Ummayah opposed the orders of the Prophet Muhammad ﷺ especially in his family and his nation as they spilt their blood, concubine their women, prison their young, destroyed their houses, destroyed their honour, and cut their offspring. They disobeyed the orders of the Prophet Muhammad ﷺ and did the opposite.

---

[41] Narrated by Ahmed as X (4/5). Hafez Ibn Hajr said in Fateh Al-Bari (13/11): Some narrations have been narrated about the cursing of Al-Hakam and his children; Narrated by At-Tabarani and others, most of it has some weakness and some are good.

[42] Narrated by Al-Bazar (6/159) and Aldiya Fi Al-Muktara (9/310-311) with Al-Hakam's name and not as X.

How will they meet the Prophet Muhammad ﷺ and what will be their state on judgment?

The ironic thing about them is that after all these crimes Mu'awiya does and the objections from the Prophet Muhammad ﷺ we still are not allowed to speak negatively of him and cannot hate him but rather he must be called our master and say May God be pleased with him.

That is how the wrong becomes right and right becomes wrong.

The scholars of Hadith and knowledge that condemned Mu'awiya were always targeted by the terrorists and would often be accused of Shi'ism and Rafidism to destroy their image in front of the public. We can see this even in our current time. This is how the true Sunnah and following the orders of Allah may be considered Rafidism and maybe even hypocrisy and disbelief in their eyes.

Some examples of scholars that were accused of Shi'ism:

Khalid Ibn Mukhled Al-Qutwani who is one of the teachers of Bukhari and Muslim narrated from him in their books. The Hafez in Tahtheeb At-Tahtheeb[43] mentioned him and said:

Ajuri Ibn Abi Dawood said: He is truthful but has some Shi'ism. Ibn Sa'ad said: He had some Shiite beliefs and only wrote from him because of necessity[44]. Al-Ejli said: Authentic and had some minor Shiite beliefs. Saleh Ibn Muhammad Jazara said: Authentic but was accused of some type of extreme belief[45].

---

[43] In Tahtheeb At-Tahtheeb (3/101)

[44] So this means they accept from these authentic people to take their religion from and take narration from them.

[45] Look how they describe him sometimes as he had some minor Shiite beliefs than was accused of some type of extreme belief and then he was an abuser

Al-Juzajani said: He was an abuser[46] announcer of his false beliefs end quote.

May Allah have mercy on you oh reader; contemplate on how they describe him sometimes as had some minor Shiite beliefs than was accused of some type of extreme belief and then Al-Juzajani the Nasibi says, He was an abuser announcer of his false belief.

---

announcer of his false belief. Hafez Ibn Hajar mentioned about Al-Juzajani in Tahtheeb (10/143): Al- Juzajani is famous for his Nasb and hatred for the family of the Prophet Muhammad ﷺ.

[46] This means he used to swear and criticise Mu'awiya.

16) THE SAYINGS OF THE GREAT SCHOLARS OF AHL AL- SUNNAH WAL JAMA'A IN CONDEMNING MU'AWIYA

There have been many scholars of Ahl al-Sunnah who have condemned Mu'awiya and we will mention some of these great scholars of Ahl al-Sunnah Wal Jama'a including An-Nas'ai author of the Sunan, Al-Hakim author of the Mustadrak, 'Abd al-Razzaq author of the Musanaf. The Imam 'Abd al-Razzaq is the teacher of the majority of the scholars of Hadith including Ahmed Ibn Hanbal, 'Ali Ibn Al-Madini (teacher of Bukhari), Muhammad Ibn Yahya At-Thuhli, Yahya Ibn Ma'een and others whom he is the teacher of all of them.

IIMAM AN-NAS'AI AUTHOR OF THE SUNAN (Died. 303H): At-Al Dahabi said in Siyar Alam An-Nubala (14/133) that An- An-Nas'ai: had some Shiite beliefs like the hatred of the enemies of 'Ali like Mu'awiya and Amr Ibn Al-Aas.

At-Al Dahabi says in Siyar Alam An-Nubala (14/132): An-Nas'ai left Egypt at the end of his life towards Damascus, where he was asked about Mu'awiya and what has been narrated about his virtues so he said: Does he not accept that we are not even mentioning him. So they continued beating him up till they removed him from the mosque. Al-Daraqutni said: He left to go to Hajj and was trialled in Damascus and achieved martyrdom.

Hafez Ibn Hajar says in Fateh Al-Bari (7/104): Many narrations about the virtues of Mu'awiya have been narrated however none are correct in terms of the chain as agreed by Ishaq Ibn Rahoya, An-Nas'ai and others.

IMAM AL-HAKIM AUTHOR OF MUSTADRAK (Died. 405H):

In Siyar Alam An-Nubala (17/175) and Tabaqat As-Shafiya for Al-Subki (4/163): When it was said to Al-Hakim to narrate some of the virtues of Mu'awiya so they may let you go. He said: It won't come from my heart meaning Mu'awiya.

IMAM 'ABD AL-RAZZAQ AUTHOR OF THE MUSANAF (Died. 211H): In Siyar Alam An-Nubala (9/570) 'Abd al-Razzaq said: Don't contaminate our lesson with the mentioning of the son of Abu Sufyan.

IMAM HAFEZ ABU GHASSAN AL-NAHDI AL-KUFEE ONE OF THE GREAT SCHOLARS OF HADITH IN ALKUFA AND FROM THE TEACHERS OF BUKHARI, ABU ZURAA, AND ABI HATIM

In Siyar Alam An-Nubala (10/432) about Abu Ghassan who is a narrator from in the six books of Hadith: Abu Ahmed Al-Hakim from Hussain Al-

Ghazi said I asked Bukhari about Abu Ghassan, he said: What exactly are you asking about? I said: His Shiite beliefs? He said: He is on the same opinion of his country. If you had seen UbaidUllah Ibn Musa or Abu Nuaim and our Kufi scholars you would not have asked me about Abu Ghassan.

I said (Al Dahabi): Abu Nuaim and UbaidUllah loved Abu Bakr and 'Umar, but they would abuse Mu'awiya and his clan.

Ubaid Ullah Ibn Musa did not allow anyone by the name of Mu'awiya to enter his house nor narrate from someone whose name was Mu'awiya as in Siyar Alam An-Nubala (9/556-557).

IMAM HAJEZ JARIR AL-DHABI (Died. 188H)

Ibn Hajar said in Tahtheeb (2/66):

Khalili said in Al-Irshad he is authentic and Qutayba said that Jarir used to abuse Mu'awiya in public.

IMAM SA'AD ALDEEN AT-TAFTAZANI AL-HANAFI (Died. 793H).

Sa'ad At-Taftazani said in Sharh Al-Maqased (5/310): That means what happened between the companions as mentioned in the books of history and on the tongues of the scholars appears that some of the companions deviated from the straight path, and reached the extent of oppression and transgression. Also caused by ignorance, jealousy, hatred, arrogance and the wanting of position and kingdom and deviance towards lust. Not all the companions are infallible nor are the people who met the Prophet Muhammad ﷺ and blessing be upon him) are necessarily good.

And what happened after to the Prophet Muhammad's ﷺ family (peace and blessing be upon them) is so clear that cannot be hidden, so devastating that there are no two opinions about it, so much that the inhabitants of the heavens and earth are weeping over it and the mountains are breaking. So may Allah's curse be upon those who participated or whoever was happy and the punishment of the hereafter is much longer and worse.

Ibn Kathir says in his Tareekh (8/224) about Yazid Ibn Mu'awiya that Mu'awiya placed as the Caliph after him:

What is narrated from the poetry of Ibn Al-Zabra in Uhud was said to have been said by Yazid:

I wish my forefathers at Badr had witnessed

How the Khazraj are by the thorns (spears) annoyed we have killed the masters of their Chiefs and equated it with Badr and it was so indeed

If Yazid actually said this then may Allah's curse be upon him. Many things have been narrated from him from crimes which he did not survive after the Hura and the murder of Al-Husain until Allah destroyed him like he destroyed the tyrants before and after him indeed he (Allah) is all-knowing all-powerful.

Ibn Kathir said in his Tareekh (8/223) upon commentating on the Hadith: Whoever instils fear upon the people of Medina; Allah will instil fear into them and curse them, he said: Scholars have used this as evidence to allow the cursing of Yazid the son of Mu'awiya. This is the narration by Ahmed Ibn Hanbal which was chosen by Al-Khalal, Abu Bakr AbdulAziz, Abu Ya'la the judge and his son Abu Hussain the Judge and was accepted by Abu Alfaraj Ibn AlJawzi in a separate book.

17) ABU SUFYAN IBN HARB, THE FATHER OF MU'AWIYA

Narrated by Muslim (2504) from Aidh Ibn Amr Ibn Al-Aas said: Abu Sufyan came to Salman, Suhaib and Bilal in the presence of a group of persons. They said: By Allah, the sword of Allah did not reach the neck of the enemy of Allah as it was required to reach.

Thereupon Abu Bakr said: Do you say this to the old man of the Quraish and their chief? Then he came to Allah's Apostle ﷺ be upon him) and informed him of this. Thereupon he (the Holy Prophet Muhammad ﷺ) said: Abu Bakr, you have perhaps annoyed them and if you annoyed them you have in fact annoyed your Lord.

So Abu Bakr came to them and said: O my brothers, I have annoyed you. They said: No, our brother, may Allah forgive you.

Al-Kawthari Al-Hanafi in Safat Al-Burhan said: And from the beliefs of this group is Comparing Allah to his creation and place, Takfeer of those who disagree and the support of the family of Harb.[47].

---

[47] The Nawasib are the supporterss of Abu Sufyan Ibn Harb. Strangely, they stand by the side of Mu'awiya which the Prophet Muhammad ﷺ said as in Bukhari (447): Ammar will be killed by the rebellious (transgressing) group. He will be inviting them (i.e., his murderers, the rebellious group) to Paradise and they will invite him to Hell-fire. This proves Sheikh Al-Kawthari was not a Nasibi but was also against Mu'awiya.

RESPONSE TO THE OPPOSING ARGUMENTS

All the narrations regarding the virtues of Mu'awiya as already mentioned previously have been rejected by major scholars of Hadith including An-Nas'ai and Ishaq Ibn Rahoya and others.

Some created some false virtues for Mu'awiya such as the Uncle of the Believers and scribe of the Quran:

The Myth of the Uncle of the Believers: Who is the one who said that Mu'awiya is the Uncle of the believers? Is it the Shariah or is it the arrogant who make up false virtues.

Did the companions call Mu'awiya Uncle of the Believers?

If Mu'awiya is the Uncle of the Believers then Huyay Ibn Aktab; the Jew and the father of Safiya would be the Grandfather of the Believers[48] The Coptics of Egypt – brothers of Mariyah Al-Qubtiya- would the Uncle of the believers too?

Ibn Kathir said in the Tafseer of (Ahzab: 6) (and his wives are their mothers):

Can we say that Mu'awiya is the uncle of the believers? The scholars have two opinions (May Allah be pleased with them). As-Shafee said: That is not said for him.

The word (not) has been removed from some of the newer editions as these editions have been altered with to change the meaning.

---

[48] This uncle is False. If it is real then why did Zubair (May Allah be pleased with him) marry Asmaa the sister of Aisha. According to that assumption, she would be his aunty and marrying your aunt is forbidden. Contemplate they will never mention that Ibn 'Umar, Abdulrahman Ibn Abi Bakr or other as Uncle of the Believers. The reason for this is that this title is only with those who are extreme supporters of Mu'awiya who is the leader of the rebellious group calling to hellfire.

The Myth (Scribe of the Quran)

We say: Scribing the Quran doesn't mean infallibility. Mu'awiya was not even a scribe of the Quran or revelation.

Where is the evidence that if someone was a scribe of the Quran then he is infallible, and that he cannot be criticized or cannot be a Fasiq or Murtad or Kafir? What can be said about an uncle this can be said too. Mu'awiya was not even a scribe of the Quran.

Ibn Abi Sarh was a scribe of the Quran. Hafez Ibn Hajar in Isabah (4/109):

Abdullah Ibn Sa'ad Ibn Abi Sarh was a scribe for the Prophet Muhammad ﷺ and the Satan deceived him and joined the Kuffar. The Prophet Muhammad ﷺ later ordered he be killed on the day of Fateh.

Narrated by Abi Dawood (4358) and An-Nas'ai (4069) and its chain is authentic.

Also narrated in Sahih Bukhari (3617) and Muslim (2781); this is the wording of Bukhari from Anas Ibn Malik (May Allah be pleased with him):

There was a Christian who embraced Islam and read Surat-al-Baqara and Al-`Imran, and he used to write (the revelations) for the Prophet Muhammad ﷺ. Later on, he returned to Christianity again and he used to say: "Muhammad ﷺ knows nothing but what I have written for him." Then Allah caused him to die, and the people buried him, but in the morning they saw that the earth had thrown his body out.

Also narrated in Ahmed (3/120) with an authentic chain and in Sahih Ibn Hiban (3/19) from Anas: There was a scribe for the Prophet Muhammad ﷺ then he left Islam and joined the polytheists and then died. The news reached the Prophet Muhammad ﷺ and said: The earth will never accept him.

Some people claim that we can't criticise Mu'awiya because of the verse, that was a nation which has passed on. It will have [the consequence of] what it earned and you will have what you have earned. You will not be asked about what they used to do. Their Interpretation is false. The blessed verse means that we will not be judged or punished for the actions of the people who passed away especially we did not commit their actions. Why would Allah forbid us to remember the past and what they did good and bad? If that was the case why did Allah tell us so many stories of Iblees, Pharoah, A'ad, Thamud, Noah, Yusuf, even up to the hypocrites up to the time of the Prophet Muhammad ﷺ We relate to you, [O Muhammad], the best of stories in what we have revealed to you of this Qur'an although you were, before it, among the unaware.

If this claim was correct, why would Allah condemn the Pharaoh and we worship Allah by reciting verses of his criticism and other verses on Abu Lahab etc? Even though they have already passed away. So now their claim with the blessed verse is incorrect.

Some narrate the Hadith of 'Umar Ibn Sa'eed said: Don't mention Mu'awiya except with good because I heard the Prophet Muhammad ﷺ say: Oh Allah guide him. Narrated by At-Tirmidhi (3843) and he weakened the narration.

Al-Albani classified it as authentic, he is wrong. Amr Ibn Al-Aas Ibn Waqid was classified as weak even by Al-Albani such as in his Daeef (2/341). Several scholars declared it weak. See Tahtheeb At-Tahtheeb (8/102) and (6/220).

5. Some of the Nawasib use this narration: Oh Allah teach him the Book and protect him from punishment.

Narrated by Ahmed (4/127) and Ibn Adi in Al-Kamil Fi Ad-Duafa (6/2402).

I said: This supplication is actually for Ibn Abbas but was fabricated and changed to Mu'awiya. In the chain is a man known as Al-Harith Ibn Ziyad who is unknown as in Tahtheeb At-Tahtheeb (2/123), Al-Mizan (1/433), which Ibn 'Abd al-Barr said: He is unknown and his narrations are strange.

This is a short and concise letter on this topic we ask Allah to make us from those who follow in good, make us from those who love and hate for the sake of Allah Almighty and make us steadfast on belief. May Allah resurrect us with his pious servants and the family of the Prophet Muhammad ﷺ and his righteous companions under the banner of the greatest Messenger Muhammad ﷺ. And praise is to Allah The Lord of the Worlds.

www.ingramcontent.com/pod-product-compliance
Lightning Source LLC
Chambersburg PA
CBHW031631040426
42452CB00007B/778
* 9 7 8 1 7 7 5 2 4 9 2 7 6 *